HOUSEPLANTS ARE FOR PLEASURE

HOUSEPLANTS

How to Grow Healthy Plants
for Home Decoration

Garden City, New York

Are for
PLEASURE

HELEN VAN PELT WILSON

DOUBLEDAY & COMPANY, INC.

ISBN: 0-385-06708-9
Library of Congress Catalog Card Number 72–97260

Printed in the United States of America

For Lucy Sargent
with Love, Admiration, and Astonishment

CONTENTS

With many thanks

To George Taloumis, who for this book has turned his skillful camera upon my houseplants.

To Charles Marden Fitch, who has enlightened me on orchids and has also patiently photographed many of my indoor plants.

To Jack Kramer, who has also increased my knowledge of orchids as well as enthusing me on small glass gardens.

To F. Gordon Foster, who has dealt sternly with every word I wrote about ferns. (He doesn't see the need for common names!)

To Elda Haring for sharing her begonia wisdom, and to Walter Haring for lending me his handsome pictures of these plants.

To Elaine Cherry for her critical reading of my chapter on fluorescent lighting, a subject on which she is expert.

To Sally Marvin, who has a way with herbs indoors and generously shared her experience with me.

To Anne Tinari, who always reads my "violet" pieces.

To Lois Wilson, who again shares her plant wisdom with me.

To William L. Meachem, managing editor of *Home Garden*, for permission to use material that appeared in that magazine over the years.

To Rachel Snyder, editor-in-chief of *Flower Grower*, for permitting me to draw on articles I had written for her magazine.

To Daniel T. Walden, whose critical—and always encouraging—reading of my manuscripts is an essential prepublication rite.

To Helen B. Krieg, whose sense of humor has not failed, as she struggled for the sixteenth time with one of my book manuscripts.

HOUSEPLANTS ARE FOR PLEASURE

I was about seven years old when my Aunt Nellie gave me my first houseplants. I potted them in an ecstasy of excitement—patient-Lucy, iceplant, geranium, coleus, and others I can't recall. I watered them with fervor and transferred them to ever larger and larger pots, for Jean, our sympathetic hired girl (in those days not called a maid), permitted this on evenings when my parents went out. Despite the oversized habitations, my plants prospered, except for the coleus, which got mealy bug, and my mother, known to her friends as Old Dutch Cleanser, firmly removed it.

Aunt Nellie's gift was the start of a lifelong hobby, pursued even through several years in a city apartment. Now in the country I have a three-exposure Plant Room. (I simply knocked out the front door and built a 9- by 11-foot addition, but more anon on this.) Plants also grow elsewhere in the house at north, south, east, and west windows, with exuberant vines at the east casements beside my breakfast table. So the count goes high, usually to 100 or more pots, and these houseplants are indeed part of my happy life.

Sometimes when a friend is bereaved or lonely—"No one needs me; it doesn't really matter whether I get up in the morning or not"—I offer a gift of plants—geraniums and wax begonias in bloom, sweet-olive for fragrance, a fast-growing philodendron, and something unfamiliar like the aromatic iboza or hardy cyclamen with its small delectable blooms, always with the warning that these need *daily* attention, preferably in the morning, and a look-over toward evening. Not for a moment do I consider that plants will be a panacea for sorrow but they can be, and usually are, a start toward looking outward, and they are a reason for daily exertion. Soon I am being called upon for advice; a new interest has been created; the original group is increased; perhaps a whole window garden is planned.

One value of houseplants is that there are kinds to suit almost every situation of light and heat. I know of none that will thrive, as sometimes advertised, "with no attention whatever," but there are some that will prosper at any but a really dark window, and for that condition there is the fun of a fluorescent light setup.

My pleasure in plants is twofold. I use them decoratively throughout my house and I particularly enjoy growing them through the months when the more demanding outdoor garden is at rest—and I am too. For indoor gardening has its limits, only so many windows, so many shelves. Outdoor enthusiasm easily goes beyond sense and strength, and the growing season sometimes turns into a marathon with me the last runner.

I grow things as common as grape-ivy and wax begonias, but every year I also order about a dozen unfamiliar plants; in time some of these become favorites as did the trailing velvet-plant, *Ruellia makoyana,* and the blue-sage, *Eranthemum nervosum,* of a few years ago; others, that don't please me or I don't please, are pitched. Perhaps you will enjoy, as I do, a different emphasis each year. Here African-violets and geraniums in their many fascinating aspects are fairly constant. But I have also become acquainted with a group of peperomias and plectranthus. Ferns, in their marvelous variety, delight me, and I always want something fragrant. The possibilities of various garden plants for indoors are also dawning upon me; recently I tried lamium, *L. galeobdolon variegatum.* Perhaps you know it as a fine groundcover, for it is winter hardy. I grow it high on a bracket and let just five well-spaced 6-foot strands develop. Unbranched, they fall straight down, making a pattern like that of an old-fashioned bead portiere. Every visitor notices this one. Such an easy plant it is, yet so exuberant and decorative, and it must have a humorous look, for everyone who sees it smiles. Well, houseplants are for pleasure!

And I hope they give you pleasure too. Remember they are to be enjoyed, not agonized over. Throw out what does not thrive; cherish what responds to your interested attention.

H.V.P.W.

Stony Brook Cottage
Westport, Connecticut
January 1973

My day begins with this happy association of plants and painting. Opposite the stairway, at the bright southern window of the Plant Room, petunias, geraniums, black-eyed-Susan vine, and cyclamens are in full bloom in a green setting of philodendron, peristrophe, and variegated tradescantia. The actors in this pageant change with the seasons but the lovely green and gold *Flora,* a fresco from an excavated villa at Stabiae, a suburb of ancient Pompeii, graces the scene throughout the year. Charles Marden Fitch photo

1

DECORATING WITH HOUSEPLANTS

Containers and Constant Color

Plants indoors offer the homemaker lively possibilities for decoration. Unlike the more permanent wallpaper and rugs, houseplants can be moved about, regrouped, interchanged. Still-life pictures can be planned to emphasize the seasons, and flower and leaf colors chosen to harmonize with furnishings. A room that is beginning to need a new paint job or some fresh upholstery can be greatly brightened and brought alive by one or two fairly large, well-chosen plants.

Pots, Baskets, Brackets, Shelves

A well-grown plant in a well-scrubbed clay pot is attractive, and a vine cascading from an indifferent plastic bowl is pleasing, but how much more decorative are plants in beautiful containers of brass, china, earthenware, gilded composition, or basketry, to name but a few possible materials, and what handsome suspended ceramics are being produced by today's imaginative potters. Then there are the wall shelves of metal or wood as suitable for plants as for ornaments or books, provided they are hung where the light is good. Library steps are another possibility.

The photographs of my container collection do not include some recent acquisitions, such as the pair of wrought-iron pedestal planters and various other items that a reader of mail-order catalogues, a visitor to ceramic shows, and a plant-minded traveler is bound to pick up.

A collection of containers and equipment to make houseplants decorative and keep them healthy. *At the left* on the window sill, the long-spouted copper watering pot (in its twenty-fifth year), plastic sprayers for misting with water or insecticides, a hygrometer-thermometer for checking temperature and humidity, and a meat baster for removing any water collecting in jardinieres. *Center and to the right,* rattan and ceramic pots and jardinieres, a pair of china pots fitted with saucers, and a big brass coal scuttle fine for a lofty begonia. Glass tables hold large and small china vessels and a wicker hanging basket (one of many). *On the floor,* on a brass trivet, an iron kettle used for a sprawling peppermint geranium, a gold paper-covered wastebasket, and a low vermilion stand, both from Japanese stores. George C. Bradbury photo

Copies of kerosene-lamp brackets—single and double black iron or brass holders—can be found at hardware stores, and these, fastened to window frames, hold pots and saucers for many trailing favorites. The luxurious green growth of hanging plants decorates my windows and makes the snowy winter landscape appear all the more beautiful.

Inexpensive brass baskets on chains, wicker cages, and Mexican baskets suspended on fine nylon cord make pleasing containers for vines. But whenever I find unusual and choice pots for other plants, they

This accumulation of years includes, *at the back,* a pair of brass birdcage planters with chains for suspension on birdcage brackets; a deep jardiniere and a ceramic for a vine, placed here on a brass English tea trivet; *in the foreground,* a white pot and a deep figured bowl (each one of a pair), a gilded pedestal Japanese bowl for the pachysandra centerpiece, a long-handled wrought-iron piece in which I plant a single bulb, and a brass three-leaf-clover stand; *along the edge,* a glass hyacinth vase, three smaller vases for cuttings, a tin pudding dish, and three yellow Japanese dishes used as pot saucers. George Taloumis photo

seem always to be porcelain and imported, at $32.50 plus tax, so I improvise. I use a pair of gilt-paper Japanese wastebaskets, 9 inches high and 8 inches across, with a block in the bottom and a rubber saucer to catch the drip, for 6-inch pots of the dramatic-foliaged *Fatsia japonica* and *Monstera deliciosa.* These have grown, almost too well, against the side walls of the big window in the Plant Room (not in front of the glass). Exuberant vines frame the picture, growing down from bracket or basket or up on wire arches (not on rickety ready-made wooden trellises).

To make these convenient arches, take two pieces of ⅛-inch galvanized wire, bend each in half to make an arch, then thrust them into the soil of a pot at right angles to each other. My tall geranium species need 60-inch wires; most jasmines and wax-plants grow around 42-inch wires, making a veritable dome of growth. Do the first twining with great care. I broke off the tip of stephanotis when fastening it to the wires

In the sunny eastern kitchen window a double black iron bracket supports two pots and saucers for lusty lamium vines, these groundcover plants lifted from the garden in September. A low leaf-shaped ceramic bowl filled with pebbles holds blooming African-violets that revel in the winter sun. Isabel Gordon photo

and it didn't speak to me for six weeks. Then it grew enthusiastically about the new supports and set flowers in summer.

Any light window or light area can be the background for a picture. In my house there are attractive plant groupings at north and west dining-room exposures, as well as at the south and east windows of Plant Room and living room. Groupings are changed through fall to spring months, depending on what I am growing—and what I am given. Friends and family know there's no gift like a plant for me, and I can always look forward to a pink cyclamen, a pink or green-white poinsettia (not reds, please) at Christmas, a lily at Easter, each proudly presented by my grandchildren. In between, pink azaleas, yellow chrysanthemums, and lavender tulips are joyfully received, and I may say if they weren't given they would be bought, for an occasional handsome flowering plant

An adjustable wrought-iron pedestal holds the common spider-plant, which here assumes an elegant air, set in a yellow plastic pot that emphasizes its own creamy variegation. It is a portable decoration thriving in light or full sun. Here it graces the west window of the dining room. George Taloumis photo

from the florist is a fine focal point among foliage plants and ferns. My enthusiasm increases for ferns. More decorative subjects hardly exist, with their varied green shadings, rhythmic frond patterns, and vigorous growth habits.

Plants need not be rare or expensive to be exciting. Consider the spider-plant, grape-ivy, tradescantia, philodendron, asparagus-fern, ever-blooming begonias, and geraniums, all absolutely foolproof, but with possibilities for excellent display. Lately I have been more and more delighted with summer annuals lifted from the garden to serve as winter houseplants. Petunias give a fine January-on performance, so too impatiens plants if frequently misted. One year I had a lovely midwinter white, pink, lavender, and purple symphony with these two plus African-violets in constant and heavy bloom. The potted seedlings of feverfew also make pleasant ferny accents through winter and produce white sprays early in March. Lantanas and pansies provide welcome notes of yellow. When the new morning-glories open their true-blue trumpets, late in February, the effect is enchanting. (More about these at the end of Chapter 11.)

Pachysandra and Ivy Cuttings

One of my most decorative houseplants, if you can call it that, is a mound of pachysandra cuttings. Inserted in a big pinholder, which is placed in a 9-inch foil cakepan with extra cuttings in the pan around the pinholder, the pachysandra makes roots and sends up pretty new pale green growth. I set the pan, concealed by the cuttings, in a footed Japanese bowl. The effect of the green planting in the gilded container is quite handsome for dining or coffee table, and certainly no trouble at all.

For constant winter color in your plant groupings, you can depend on wax begonias, geraniums, and African-violets. I particularly enjoy my African-violets the first thing in the morning because I set the timer on the fluorescents to light up before I do. Incidentally, one very early morning when I didn't light up quite early enough and was measuring both instant coffee and liquid fertilizer, there was a near disaster, for I almost drank the wrong thing. I am more careful now and, if I am also preparing Jell-O, I know I must have my mind going three ways, not just one on my houseplants.

Just as easy—and as pleasing—is English ivy, short pieces used like the pachysandra, long sprays in a vase. They root in either situation; just be sure to cut by early August before growth hardens. I put mine in a pail of water on the porch so they will be ready for me before frost.

Needless to say, houseplants to be decorative must be at peak of perfection, and do be assured there is nothing sinful about discarding unsightly specimens or those that bore you through too long residence.

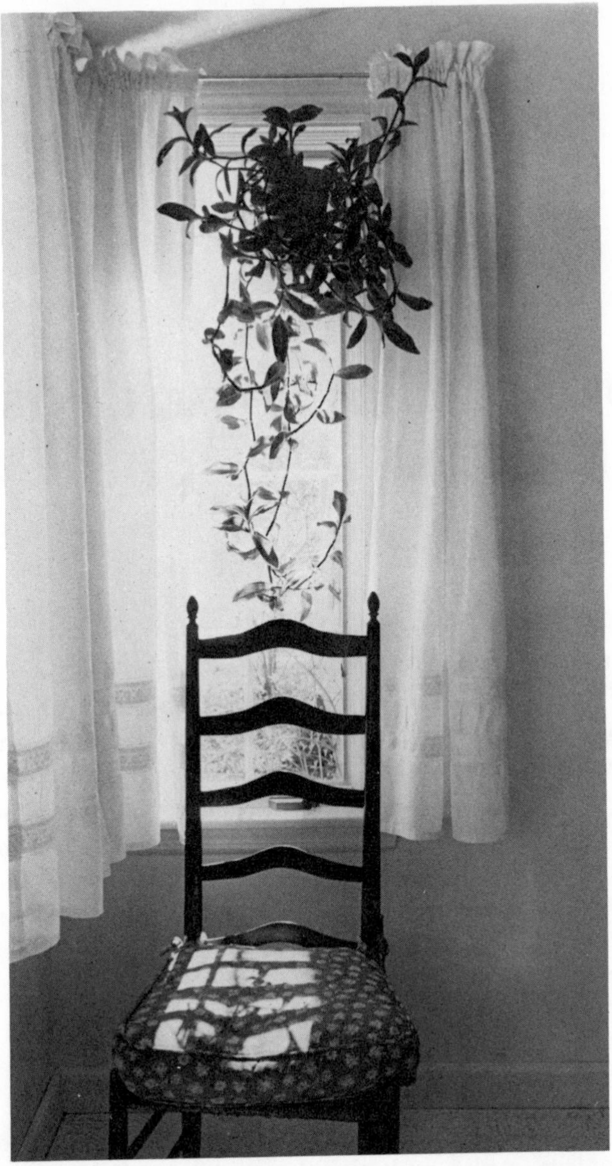

Supported by a single lamp-bracket fixture, one plant of a purple-green tradescantia decorates another kitchen window in November, and it grows and grows and grows all winter until by May it is a thrifty 3 feet long. Isabel Gordon photo

2

THE WIDE WORLD OF HOUSEPLANTS

Our Global Possibilities

It did not occur to me that my world of houseplants was so wide until I took a count one winter that added up to 147. My trouble is that I read mail-order catalogues at night, which results in morning ordering of so many plants that they overflow into living and dining rooms, even guest rooms. But the house looks happy in winter and so am I, devoting a half hour each morning (and other little oddments of time, I'm sure) and one weekend morning to my plants. It is interesting that species that come from diverse regions of the globe can be grown so successfully in our homes. Sometimes it helps to know their habitats but even then we can accommodate their preferences only to a certain degree.

Pleasant Miscellany

You need not concentrate on only a few kinds to have beautiful indoor effects. Unlike outdoor garden beds that look spotty with too many kinds, indoor gardens can be achieved on a one-of-each basis, since pots and planters seem to provide a unifying element. I do not keep the same plants year after year. Some outgrow the house and are given to friends with larger quarters or to institutions; many, like the big geraniums, become terrace plants; only the vines, a few foliage plants, the African-violets, and certain choice unusual things remain. Then there are my

This Thanksgiving still life at one end of the broad window sill in the living room—where decorations are changed most frequently—includes a dependable zygocactus (it blooms again at Easter), a footed bowl of narcissus bulbs on their way to Christmas fragrance and beauty, and a blue Victorian vase of English ivy sprays, with a favorite art book and a favorite Annunciation to set the scene. George Taloumis photo

selections from those that are marked in the catalogues "for greenhouse only." What can the greenhouse offer that I with effort cannot? I ask, and sometimes, alas, I find out. The acacia did not care for home life here, but the lovely bouvardia bloomed fragrantly through fall to winter and set buds again in summer. That is a "greenhouse" plant I will always cherish.

People are amused to see me growing such "common" plants as philodendron, grape-ivy, spider-plant, and large and small specimens of *Asparagus sprengeri* (not *A. plumosus,* whose habits are not neat). On occasion, the sprengeri produces scented blooms and then red berries. I have a big specimen on a little marble-topped Victorian table

The winter still life in the sunny living room now includes a tall lavender petunia (in the corner), a white-flowering Swedish-ivy below it, trivets of African-violets on two levels, and on the sill a large coral 'Firebird' coleus, its handsome foliage set off by the gilt ceramic jardiniere. George Taloumis photo

in the Plant Room; there to my eyes it has an elegant air. In the kitchen in some years a smaller plant cascades from one side of a double iron bracket, from the other side a trailing grape-ivy is allowed to wander across the east window. In a brass birdcage at the north casement, the philodendron knows no bounds, and a peppermint geranium at the south end smells minty when the sun shines on it or I deliberately bruise a leaf or two to enjoy the stimulating herbal aroma.

Well known also but none the less interesting to me is the crown-of-thorns, *Euphorbia splendens.* This Madagascan is something of a climber with red flowers, tiny bright green leaves, and many sharp thorns. Grown in sandy soil, kept on the dry side, and in full sun, it is practically never out of bloom. A bent-wire coat hanger inserted in the pot gives direction

The spring still life in the living room features a white cyclamen in a gilt ceramic jardiniere. The plant—received before Christmas and kept wet and cool at this window with no storm sash—opens buds well into May. Accompanying it are a blue Tiffany vase of forced yellow forsythia, a pink azalea in a woven tan pot-cover, a large pink impatiens plant, and the broad-leaved amaryllis, a handsome contrasting foliage plant now that its great lily bloom is gone. On the latch strip a small plant of the trailing begonia 'Ivy Ever' completes the picture. Charles Marden Fitch photo

to its brambly habit. Less common is the fragrant blue biennial German-violet, *Exacum affine,* actually from Socotra Island south of Arabia.

Variegated foliage plants also enliven the winter picture. Mine are mainly green and white—from China and Japan, *Daphne odora* 'marginata' (and the green daphne, too, both blooming fragrantly in winter); the Greek myrtle, *Myrtus communis,* slow and handsome for a bracket;

the West Indian basket-grass, *Oplismenus,* a mound of arching pink, green, and white ribbons; variegated peperomias, dwarf and standard; 'Gold Leaf' tradescantia, several small-leaved ivies, and that beautiful evergreen from China, *Pittosporum tobira* 'variegata.' It bears cream-yellow flowers in winter and they have a delectable orange-blossom scent.

To increase winter color I bring in from the cool garage where they have been rooting a series of French-Roman hyacinths grown in bowls of pebbles and water. I introduce a few such long-blooming florist plants as rosy cyclamens, pink poinsettias, yellow marguerites, and lavender primroses. Gift plants of pink or white azaleas I hold over year after year, for they are indeed spectacular houseplants. From March into April—three to five weeks—I also enjoy the regal or Lady Washington geraniums. The Paperwhite narcissus parade through the winter months.

Four Not to Miss

A shrubby plant I must always have is the Mexican blue-sage, *Eranthemum nervosum.* This species produces deep, true-blue, not purple, spikes in winter when any flowers are welcome but especially those in a color so rare among houseplants. This is fast-growing in full sun and likes a lot of water. The second year mine grew to 30 inches and required a 6-inch pot. Then on a stand of its own, it dominated the Plant Room. It is colorful in summer, too. When it was small, I found that if I put it under lights I could speed up formation of the next set of bloom as one set ended.

The so-called Egyptian star-cluster, *Pentas lanceolata,* pink, white, or lavender, blooms through the year given full sun, plenty of water and fertilizer, and humidity to 50 per cent or more. If my plants start getting yellow leaves in winter, I cover them with perforated plastic bags for a couple of weeks and the increased humidity brings back their looks. Pentas are newcomers to us from tropical Africa and Arabia, and jewels that everyone admires. Mine grow to about 15 inches and are nipped back to promote bushy flowering branches. At a window in winter and on the stone platform at the front door with geraniums in summer, they are charming plants.

The trailing velvet-plant, *Ruellia makoyana,* from Brazil has rather restrained procumbent growth and silver-veined foliage flushed rose. Small brilliant cerise trumpets are produced through the year except for about eight weeks in summer. Late in winter this is a delightful com-

Above left, the apostle-plant, *Neomarica gracilis,* bears fragrant high-up irislike blooms and also two between the new foliage fans that develop far down at the ends of curving leaves. *Above right,* the Egyptian star-cluster, *Pentas lanceolata,* pink, white, or lavender, blooms throughout the year; *below,* the miniature cyclamen, *C. neapolitanum,* is an enchanting 5-inch replica of the familiar larger type. Merry Gardens photos

panion at a west window for a paler pink baby cyclamen, *Cyclamen neapolitanum,* the one that grows so abundantly in the wild from France to Greece. If I can induce you to try but one unusual houseplant, let it be this treasure.

This miniature cyclamen, an endearing 5-inch replica of my taller

Above left, the so-called German-violet from Asia, *Exacum affine,* is biennial with a heavy crop of scented lavender-blue winter flowers that look rather like African-violets. *Above right,* this handsome evergreen from China, *Pittosporum tobira* 'variegata,' flourishes at a north window while growing slowly to miniature tree form and producing cream-yellow winter flowers of fine orange-blossom fragrance. *Below left,* the crown-of-thorns, *Euphorbia splendens,* is almost never out of bloom, the small red flowers dotting the bright green leaves with no harm from the terrible sharp thorns that cover the branches. *Below right,* the upright, everblooming white Cape-primrose, a streptocarpus hybrid, is both beautiful and easy. Merry Gardens photos favorite, seems to bloom off and on throughout the year, most perhaps in summer and fall, but it does not need a dry rest like the familiar florist cyclamen; just a quiet time late in spring. Now in a 3½-inch pot, it spreads gracefully well beyond the pot rim. In summer it is a cause of admiration on an end table on the porch. It is deep pink but there is also a white form. When a seed pod is forming, the stem makes a tight little spiral like a corkscrew. If you admire the big *C. persica,* you will be entranced by this baby cyclamen, especially if your space for flowering plants is limited. (Watch for scale, easy to pick off when the first few appear.)

Iboza riparia rivals Jack's beanstalk for speed. In a few months this South African plant in a 3-inch pot will fling out 3- to 4-foot corky stems with aromatic leaves. Long fluffy sprays of cream-white flowers open in late February and keep coming for eight to ten weeks. It is not for small quarters but a delight if you have room for it.

With iboza, I grow the Swedish-ivy, *Plectranthus oertendahlii* 'variegatus,' a fleshy creeper from Australia, not Sweden. It blooms about the same time as iboza with similar but shorter sprays of pink-white flowers but it produces so many white-marbled leaves, it appears to be always in full bloom. In a sunny window I also enjoy a variegated upright form.

Coming from our Rocky Mountains, the prairie-mallow, *Malvastrum coccineum,* grows to 12 inches and is long-blooming with coral-pink flowers and feathery, sharply indented, gray-green leaves, a graceful ornament for basket or bracket.

And so I continue to try plants I haven't grown before. Right now I seem to be on my way, *reluctantly,* I admit, with orchids. And these are a whole wide world of their own.

3

GREEN IS ALSO A COLOR

Ferns and Other Foliage Favorites

As in nature, the garden in the house is framed and accented with green. We all want flowers of various colors, but green is also a color and valuable as a foil for flowers. Once we *see* green as hue, we begin to appreciate the great variety of shades and then of leaf forms and textures that occur in our choice foliage plants. Consider ferns. These offer a wide range of coloring and frond shape.

FERNS. Looking around at the ferns growing here, I again admire their beauty and rejoice in their simple cultural needs. Mine flourish in fully light situations, mainly at north and west windows because there is more room there. Ferns also like the pale winter sunshine. When this gets strong in March, I find it wise to diffuse the light through the partly slatted venetian blind.

Heat, Humidity, and Drainage

A temperature not much above 70 degrees is preferred and I find ferns also flourish at a fairly steady 68 degrees. As for humidity, most of them aren't really so demanding as is claimed. The few in the Plant Room thrive on the pebble trays and humidity there runs 45 to 70 per cent. If grown in groups, they make their own humidity. If placed separately,

Decoration for a south bedroom window. The delicate pale green maidenhair fern is set off by a white ceramic jardiniere placed on a Directoire table beside a blue-and-white French chair. Certain plants seem to suit definite periods and color schemes, but the maidenhair fern looks beautiful and grows well in any light place. A venetian blind mitigates the sun's glare. George Taloumis photo

Green is also a color in all its fascinating variations, as you can see, in this collection of ferns, vines, and other foliage plants that flourish without sun but in the bright light of the north dining-room window. Charles Marden Fitch photo

syringe the tops frequently at the sink. Because they are so attractive, I display many of them in glazed or gilded ceramic pots, and to make the most of my collection on a table at a north window, I set the big holly fern at the back on a brass tripod, letting more light in on the small ones in front.

My ferns are potted in compost, mainly decayed leaves, lightened with a little sand. Garden soil with plenty of humus and some perlite will do as well. When they are in active growth—they don't move much from November to February—I feed my ferns along with the other houseplants. Fish-oil emulsion is a fertilizer recommended by experts.

Good drainage in the pot is the absolute essential; if this is reliable, you can hardly overwater. My ferns are watered almost daily to provide an evenly moist but not too wet condition. The tops are infrequently syringed but often enough to keep them clean. If your ferns, like mine, are in decorative outer pots, do be careful about letting water collect. The *inverted* saucer in the bottom is one safeguard; frequent examination is another.

Don't be disturbed by the browning of the lower foliage on some kinds; just cut it off. The only pest I've had is scale, once on the stems of the big davallia and once on the birds-nest. Discovered at the start, scale is easy to pick off; it is not to be confused with the sporangia (clusters of spores) or some sori (little mounds or disks of spore cases). On the underside of the fronds the sori of the birds-nest fern form parallel lines; those of the pellaeas and brakes are marginal. If scale gets ahead of you, give your plant a *weak* malathion dip.

Many Favorites

I hardly know where to start when describing my favorite ferns. I've grown so many through the years and all with such pleasure. Of course, the names are terrible but when you order you have to use them, for one man's hares-foot may be another's squirrel- or deer-foot.

I am particularly fond of two of the davallias. The big one, called rabbits-foot, *Davallia fejeensis,* with 18-inch fronds, is fine for a hanging basket; for me it grows as a graceful pedestal plant; the dwarf *D. f. plumosa* makes a pretty table piece in a low clay dish. It's the furry brown rhizomes stretching over the pot rims that have resulted in the odd descriptive names for the davallias. Pegged down, the rhizomes root at various places and can be cut off and separately potted to give you more plants.

The maidenhairs, *Adiantum,* are choice and happy with more sunlight than the others. The pendant fan-maidenhair, *A. tenerum* 'Wrightii,' is lovely in a jardiniere on a little table, and small specimens can be grown, as I have them, on a window shelf. I also have the compact, darker green upright *A. hispidulum;* it is attractive but not graceful like 'Wrightii.'

The sturdy Japanese holly-fern, *Cyrtomium falcatum* 'Rochefordianum,' with crisp, glossy, wavy fronds, pointed like holly leaves, is a good contrast to the feathery davallias and maidenhairs, and I like the birds-nest fern, *Asplenium nidus,* for its lighter green and smooth, quite different texture and growth form.

The sword ferns—the familiar Boston, *Nephrolepis exaltata,* with

Ferns, interesting and dependable, are appreciated for their varying shades of green, differences of form, and contrasts in texture. *Left,* the silver-green Victorian brake; *right,* a lacy version of the Boston fern. Merry Gardens photos

drooping fronds is one—now appear in many forms. Hardly swordlike is 'Fluffy Ruffles' or the dwarf 'Verona.'

The big and little leatherleafs—*Polystichum* (*Rumohra*) *adiantiforme* and the compact *P. tsus-simense,* small enough for a bubble garden—and the forms of *Pteris,* the brake or table ferns, especially *P. ensiformis* 'Victoriae,' the Victorian brake, are well worth growing. And don't overlook the two or three ferns that may come with your Christmas poinsettia. They are probably cultivars of *Pteris cretica.* Plant them separately in small pots and they will flourish for you.

Pellaea hastata adorns the summer porch but hardly fills me with rapture indoors in winter, for it rests until February, and if forced before then, it forms new fronds that brown at the tips. Perhaps you will like as much as I do the tall blue-gray *Polypodium aureum glaucum,* called hares-foot, for no resemblance that I can see, but maybe I've never been close enough to a hare. You may want to try the forked, pendant staghorn fern that friends of mine grow so dramatically mounted on wood. This one, nice for an enclosed porch, is something of a challenge, requiring more humidity than the others.

If you want to plant a dish garden or terrarium with ferns, it is better to select those that stay small rather than to try big growers in small sizes. A good selection would be the small davallia, one of the table ferns like 'Wilsonii,' and the button fern, *Pellaea rotundifolia.* Bronzy green fronds only a few inches long make the tiny *Cheilanthes gracillima* ideal. And in small plantings you could use one of the charming club-mosses or *Selaginella kraussiana brownii* with its fluffy growth.

Not ferns, but so called, the airy *Asparagus plumosus,* which I don't care for—perhaps I have seen it "softening" too many florists' bouquets —and *A. sprengeri,* the needle asparagus which I dote on, are very easy. This last is a plant to which I really give house room, but even so I keep it to a 9-inch pot by root slicing (Chapter 4). If you set it outside in summer, the bright red berries, falling on the ground, germinate and make adorable youngsters for next winter's windows.

OTHER GREEN FAVORITES. The choice among fine foliage plants is infinite but I have space here for only so many of the big ones. On each side of the long tray in the Plant Room, against paneling, not windows, and over the radiators, but lifted on a footed lacquer stand, I have grown the ferny-foliaged, red-brown, metallic false-aralia, now called by the mouthful, *Dizygotheca elegantissima.* Actually a small tree, it can grow to 25 feet, but I find it another home after 3 feet when it begins to conceal the wall painting of *Flora* from ancient Stabiae. (I do enjoy combining my two enthusiasms of plants and paintings.) The ivy-aralia cross, called three-ivy, *Fatshedera lizei,* with star-shaped leaves is another nice tall one.

The Norfolk-Island-pine, *Araucaria excelsa,* is a house evergreen that can be kept to about 3 feet and trimmed as a delightful small Christmas tree, nice for an apartment. Then there are the aspidistras, dracaenas, rubber-plants, and the umbrella-tree, *Schefflera actinophylla,* all of which will thrive with some indirect daylight.

Among smaller foliage subjects is the familiar piggyback-plant, *Tolmiea menziesii,* with soft overlapping leaves; it makes nice moundy growth, the new plants growing on top of the old. Then there are the peperomias. I got going on these one year, selecting four out of twenty-eight listed in one catalogue, and I still grow two of the vining ones—*Peperomia fosteriana* and *P. scandens variegatus* 'Royal Gold.'

Choice Variegated Plants

Plants with colorful foliage add life to an all-green tapestry. Although variegation is more pronounced in sunshine, there is also a fair amount in full light. The prayer-plant, *Maranta leuconeura kerchoveana,* maintains the maroon markings on its gray-green leaves in any light place. This is the one that folds its leaves at night, a habit that can be quite alarming to a plant-sitter; my daughter, caring for my plants in my absence, was sure this furling was but the forerunner of demise. The

Left, the false-aralia with its metallic sheen is a handsome dignified plant with arresting leaf form, good for contrast among bushy growers. (Alas, it outgrew me.) George C. Bradbury photo. *Right,* the Norfolk-Island-pine, an excellent house evergreen, is easily kept to 3 feet by pruning. In an apartment, it can be trimmed with ornaments to serve as a Christmas tree. Merry Gardens photo

prayer-plant looks particularly nice on the summer porch where it is suspended in a terra-cotta basket. The so-called silver-leaf maranta, *Calathea argyraea,* gray-green and silvery, is another lovely variegated.

Indispensable for me is the spider-plant. It has much too much elegance to be so easy and it does not sulk in a dim place. However, it won't let down any ladders of little plants without full light. The green and white spider-plant is *Chlorophytum comosum,* the one with yellow-centered ribbon leaves, *C. c. picturatum.* I grow them as shelf, basket, and pedestal plants, and my immediate neighborhood is evidence of my enthusiasm and the prolific tendencies of these plants.

The upright, purple-tinted velvet-plant, *Gynura aurantiaca,* offers pleasant color contrast, and *G. sarmentosa,* a procumbent grower, makes an excellent window-garden accent when elevated on an inverted flower pot, perhaps with pink wax begonias on each side. Gynura also produces bloom but I prize it for foliage alone; it has about the ugliest flowers I've ever seen—small yellow paintbrushes; I cut them off at once.

The distinguished *Coleus blumei* 'Firebird' brings bright tints of yellow and orange to the window shelves; I will always want it and I have never given cuttings to a friend who hasn't prized this one. But most coleuses make colorful window plants, and a number of small plants in preferred colors are worth lifting from the garden. I have some unnamed green and gold ones that I like because they emphasize the yellow note in all my decorations. Repeated through a window garden, like accent plants in a garden, they give a sense of design to the picture.

The aucubas, aphelandras, columneas, episcias, and fittonias offer further attractions. If you read the houseplant catalogues as I do, you will discover a surprising wealth of variegated plants so that your indoor gardens in light without sun will still seem to be in bloom.

4

THE COMFORTABLE HOUSEPLANT

Soils, Potting, and Fertilizing

You can be extremely fancy about the soil or "growing medium" for your plants or extremely plain. Mine is the plain policy. I grow practically everything in some variation of the old Equal-Thirds Mixture:

1 part soil from a well-worked garden bed
1 part compost or other humus
1 part sharp clean sand (builders', not seashore sand) or perlite

Thus, for ferns and begonias, I use mainly compost with just a little sand. The compost comes from one of my big rotted leaf piles. It is sifted through a ½-inch sieve and is just nice and crumbly. Geraniums here get about half and half compost and sand, the African-violets almost all compost (no nematodes in this area) and, if I were growing desert cacti, which I am not, I'd allow at least two parts sand to one part humus.

Generally speaking, houseplants are far less finicky than you may have been led to believe. Roots need support and plants need nourishment but you don't have to stew over formulas unless you are growing show plants. Then it is worth while to be as particular as are most exhibitors and specialists.

For instance, you may want to prepare or buy ready-made an organic mix like Nature's Way for your African-violets. If you are particular enough to make up an ideal growing medium just for your geraniums, you will find one given in Chapter 9. I have used several of the commercial mixtures that come in bags but always with some coarsening additive and also a little charcoal. I have found that mixes "as is" are generally too light, but they are weed-free and pest-free, very convenient, especially if you have to do any repotting in winter or live in an apartment with no garden soil available.

For Apartment Dwellers

Also useful for the apartment dweller are the artificial soil mixes for container plants. These follow the formulas of the famous Cornell Mixes usually called peat-lite. You can prepare this peat-lite mix yourself (but what a job) or buy it ready to use under a trade name like Jiffy-Mix, Redi-Earth, or Parks Sure-Fire Mix. Basically this is the Cornell formula:

½ bushel (4 gallons) Terra-Lite vermiculite (No. 2 grade)
½ bushel (4 gallons) shredded sphagnum peat
4 tablespoons 20 per cent superphosphate (powdered)
8 tablespoons ground limestone (or calcium carbonate)
Either but not both of these:
6 tablespoons 33 per cent ammonium nitrate OR 1 cup 5-10-5 fertilizer

Mix dry in a large garbage can. Store dry in a large plastic bag or the can. Moisten a few hours before using. Makes 1 bushel.

Artificial soil for acid-requiring plants—azalea, camellia, citrus, gardenia, sweet-olive, epiphyllum cactus

1 bushel shredded sphagnum peat
¼ ounce (1 teaspoon) potassium nitrate
¾ ounce (4 teaspoons) 20 per cent superphosphate
2 ounces (3½ tablespoons) dolomite lime
3¾ ounces (6 tablespoons) calcium carbonate lime

This may be stored indefinitely if dry; it has a pH of about 5.7 depending on the quality of the peat. Makes 1 bushel.

These are lightweight mixtures. Tall, heavy plants potted in them need holding down. Polished stones or small rocks make an attractive weighty mulch for the topsoil, and clay rather than plastic pots are indicated. About two months after potting, you will want to start applying a soluble fertilizer.

Pots—Kinds and Sizes

Plants thrive in almost any containers provided they are of suitable size for the root systems and have drainage holes. It takes a lot of experience and care to water plants properly if there are no outlets. True, you can provide an extra layer of drainage material in a pot without a drain but you will still be likely to overwater. I know I am inclined to. (If I see a plant ailing in a jardiniere, I am pretty likely to find it standing in water.)

Clay or plastic pots are both acceptable. Plants in clay pots require more water than those in plastic because of evaporation through the clay walls. Ceramists are now making one-of-a-kind pots and, provided these have outlets, they are both pretty and useful. If they are large enough, you can use them as jardinieres rather than for direct potting. I particularly like the well-designed containers suspended by cords or chains and am grateful when they come my way as Christmas gifts.

I use all kinds of pots but more, I notice, of the plastic type. I like their soft colors and the fact that fertilizer doesn't discolor them as it does clay. Nor is a collection of salts as likely to build up on the rims.

When you buy plants by mail order, they usually arrive in 2-, 2¼-, or 2½-inch pots, depending on the type of plant and also on the grower. (Orchids are an exception, a law unto themselves; all of my last order came in 3's.) Don't be in a hurry to shift plants on to roomier quarters. If you buy them in fall and fertilize them through winter, you may not need to repot until spring. In any case, let them first recover from the rigors of travel, and be assured that a larger pot is rarely a panacea for poor health. Usually there is some other cause. Some people have a great enthusiasm for repotting and are always *at* their plants, but I loathe the whole messy business and so keep my plants in small pots as long as possible, counting on almost daily feeding, in small portions, to meet their needs.

Repotting

You can do the big repotting job when you take plants out in spring or about a month before you bring them in in fall. Depending on their looks—size, color of leaves, etc.—I repot some at both seasons, but more in spring, and do not necessarily shift to larger containers. It is better not to repot at all than to move a plant into a container that is much too large for it. (Too much soil produces a kind of plant indigestion.)

Usually you can settle for a pot one size larger than the one in which a plant has been growing.

If a plant is not potbound, that is, roots are not creeping out of the drainage hole at the bottom or winding around the outside of the earth ball, simply replace any loose old soil with fresh and reset the plant in the same pot. With large hard-to-handle specimens, you may be able to scrape away the worn topsoil, filling in with a rich fresh mixture, and so avoid depotting altogether. If a plant looks sickly and you find roots soft, cut them back, reduce top growth as well, and return the plant to the same pot, or even to a smaller one; in either case provide fresh soil. (Or discard the plant.)

With indefatigable growers like my asparagus-fern, which would fill a room if I shifted it on every year as the heavy roots indicate, I follow a drastic procedure. I slice off an inch or so of the lowest roots and also run a sharp knife an inch around the outer area of the root ball. In this way I hold my plant to a 9-inch pot and that's as big as I care to have it.

Of course, pots must be clean. Scrub the old ones with hot soapy water, using a scouring pad for encrusted rims. If pots are in bad condition, soak them overnight—or throw them out. Some just aren't worth the effort of cleaning. Soak *new* clay pots for hours until they have taken up all the water they can hold; otherwise they will draw unduly from the soil and for a time you will have trouble keeping soil moist enough.

Let plants dry out a little before repotting; it makes them easier to handle. To depot a plant, slide your left hand over the top of the pot with the plant stem between first and second fingers. Grasping the edge of the pot lightly, turn it upside down, and tap the rim firmly against the edge of step or table. Out should come plant and soil, all in one piece, to be neatly shifted elsewhere without broken roots. If a plant doesn't loosen after a hard knock or two, with your right hand push the blunt end of a pencil through the drainage hole. That usually separates soil and pot neatly. Sometimes a pot must be broken to get it off; this happens when repotting has been neglected and a heavy mass of roots crowds the pot.

When you pot a plant in either a clay or plastic container, take care of drainage requirements. Put an *arching* piece of "crock," which is a bit of broken clay pot, over the drainage hole to slow but not stop the outflow of water. One piece will suffice for a small pot. In 4-inch or larger sizes, arrange a layer of crocking above the single piece, and then spread a thin layer of gravel, small driveway stones, or sphagnum moss

Raid

Raid

Raid

if you have it. I save the moss packing that comes with new plants for this purpose. Such an arrangement keeps soil from washing down and clogging the drainage hole, and also retards outflow just enough. It isn't good to have water rushing through soil so fast it is not properly moistened. Also there are spills from overflowing pot saucers.

With drainage material in place, sprinkle a little soil over it, center the plant, and fill in with more soil. Firm it with a stick, ruler, or piece of lath to get soil in good contact with roots. Strike the pot sharply on the potting table as you work to firm the soil.

However, the ideal is not a cemented condition, just a comfortably firm one to encourage sturdy, stocky growth. When soil is too loose or too spongy because of excess humus or inadequate firming, growth may be soft and sappy and flowering poor. Try to set the plant a little deeper than before, and do leave space to receive water at the top, ½ inch in a small pot, 1 inch or more in a large one. Nothing is more aggravating than a plant potted so high that when watering you have to go back to it several times since so much of each application flows down the sides of the pot.

Fertilizing—How Much and When

The kind of plant food you use, the amount, and the time of application all depend on the medium—the soil or soilless mix—in which plants are growing, also, of course, whether they are in a quiet period in winter, as summer-flowering campanulas might be, or have just finished

Plans for Potting. *Above,* a newspaper is spread over the 3-foot-high trash box, a comfortable height for working. Here are plants needing repotting, pots of various sizes, stones and broken pot "crocks," a ruler for a potting stick, and packages of plant food and charcoal. *Center left,* a plant is eased from the pot, the rim struck sharply against the edge of the box to loosen the earth ball. *Center right,* soil is loosened from the tangle of roots to make room for fresh soil and a one-size-larger pot. *Below left,* a piece of arched crocking is fitted over the drainage hole to retain water long enough to moisten soil but let it out fast enough to prevent sogginess. *Below right,* when annuals are lifted from a garden bed, they usually require severe cutting back although some growth must remain to nourish plants while new roots form. Here the long branch of a petunia is cut back as far as the low clustered foliage. Moved to the porch for the fall weeks, then indoors in late September, it grew and bloomed from January on. George Taloumis photos

Drastic procedure for a too large sprenger asparagus. *Above,* every year more than an inch is cut away from around the root ball and also across the bottom. *Below,* returned to the *same* pot with some fresh soil tamped down with a ruler, the plant is not resentful and continues to be a strong accent for the marble-topped table in the Plant Room. The pail holds soil from the compost pile mixed with a little sand. It is refilled, and kept covered in the garage for emergency repotting in winter. George Taloumis photos weeks of heavy budding and blooming, like your winter geraniums. My own policy is to feed lightly *with every watering* except in periods of rest or of prolonged dull or rainy weather when plants can't use much food since there is no sun for the process of photosynthesis (the manufacture of food in the presence of light). I mix the solution with a "pinch" of the dry material to my 2-quart watering can, and that is about quarter strength.

I like the soluble fertilizers—Peters various brands, Stim-u-plant, Plant Marvel, Hyponex, Black Magic, and Rapid-Gro. I don't depend on one brand, even if it is "complete." Balance of elements varies with the different formulas so I usually keep three going each winter. Some of you may also like to feed alternately with an organic fish emulsion. I give the acid-preference plants—gardenia, sweet-olive, pittosporum, and others—a monthly dose of something like Miracid to maintain acidity. Occasional watering with a vinegar solution—½ teaspoon to 1 quart of water—also promotes acidity.

In discussing or buying fertilizers, a number of terms are used which may not be familiar to you. Here are a few explanations.

ORGANIC FERTILIZERS are those composed of once-living matter, such as fish emulsion, animal manure, blood, or bone meal; or decayed vegetable residues—grass, leaves, stems, hay, cottonseed meal.

INORGANIC FERTILIZERS are chemical products, artificially manufactured—nitrate of soda, ammonium sulfate, muriate of potash, and superphosphate.

COMMERCIAL FERTILIZERS are packaged or bagged products usually containing both organic and inorganic materials (with, if they are good, a fair amount of organic matter). Often this quantity is indicated, as "40 per cent of the nitrogen from organic sources." Percentages of the vital elements are indicated, as 15-30-15, meaning 15 per cent nitrogen, 30 per cent phosphorus, and 15 per cent potash. The remaining 40 per cent is an inert carrier with little or no fertility.

NITROGEN promotes leaf and stem strength and stimulates growth generally. Too much makes plants spindly and poor at flower production, inclined to bud drop. An excess may turn variegated foliage back to plain green.

PHOSPHORUS is for roots. It also gives a steady push to flower and seed production. Too little results in poor foliage color. Too much makes growth sappy, lacking in fiber, so that the plant has a floppy look. Bone meal is a good source. Allow 1 teaspoon to each 5-inch pot of soil.

POTASH is the antitoxin among plant foods. It wards off disease, stabilizes growth, and intensifies color. Lacking it, a plant has a dull look; flowers have no luster. Wood ashes are one source. Their strength varies with different woods. A 5-inch potful to 1 bushel of soil is safe.

THE THREE ELEMENTS—nitrogen, phosphorus, and potash—form the basis for all "balanced" houseplant fertilizers. While it is possible to buy packages of each element, it is infinitely easier to purchase them mixed in appropriate amounts.

"TRACE ELEMENTS"—iron, boron, manganese, and others—in small amounts are also necessary to healthy plant life. As a rule these are present in all growing mediums.

Do not feed ailing plants unless you have every reason to believe they are starving. Usually sick plants are suffering from almost anything except lack of food. Maybe humidity or light or watering is at fault. If for no apparent reason healthy plants fail to bloom, try this treatment: Once each week apply a solution of 1 teaspoon superphosphate to 1 gallon of water. If, after six weeks, no buds are visible, something else must be wrong, for your plants are certainly not starving.

It is a good idea to withhold food for a week or so after a big bout of blooming. Most plants have peaks and valleys of flowering. They require a little peace and quiet after production in order to gather their resources again. They should not be urged too quickly from their rest, or allowed to rest too long.

SOIL CONDITIONERS. Certain materials other than fertilizers are essential components of soils suitable for various plants. Most houseplants will thrive in a neutral or slightly acid or slightly alkaline soil. Some *prefer* a higher percentage of one or the other, and a few suffer seriously unless the medium is strongly acid or strongly alkaline according to their need. For these, the soil conditioners, lime (alkaline) and aluminum sulfate, sulfur, or tannic acid (all three acid) should be added, but carefully and only as directed.

There are on the market commercial preparations, such as Miracid, to maintain the desired pH reading. I use this once a month on acid-preference plants: chrysanthemums, gardenia, sweet-olive, pittosporum, azaleas, and all other members of the heath family. Few houseplants need a really alkaline soil, asparagus, mignonette, and maidenhair being three. Most ferns like a neutral or just slightly acid soil.

PERLITE OR SPONGE-ROK is one of the useful additives to soil mixes; it is lightweight, a sterile form of volcanic rock; the white, spongy pellets aerate the soil. Sometimes these are confused with soil mealy bugs, but perlite pellets don't move; mealy bugs do. In some areas, perlite is easier to obtain than the desired amounts of sand.

VERMICULITE, sterile mica rock, also lightweight, is another excellent soil conditioner holding quantities of water, rather too much for African-violets. Alone it provides a good medium for seeds or rooting leaves.

SPHAGNUM MOSS is a bog plant, useful to cover the drainage layer in pots; it can also be used alone as a growing medium provided a soluble fertilizer is added regularly since sphagnum moss has no food value. Sphagnum peat is the moss in a state of partial decay, light brown in color, a good source of humus.

5

DAY BY DAY IN EVERY WAY

Seven Keys to Success

Regular attention is the absolute essential for success with houseplants, and I take that for granted as I key the other needs, for potted plants indoors are entirely dependent on *your* care. Rains don't cover up neglect, and to avoid starvation, roots can't forage as in a garden bed.

1. PROVIDE LIGHT OR SUN. Most plants will thrive in a fully light situation; only a few will grow where it is dim. (Apparently my spider-plant doesn't mind, though it didn't make offsets until I moved it from a dark corner, where it was decorative, to a bright window.) The majority of small foliage plants will *endure* a week or so away from light on coffee table, dining table, or mantel, or on the floor if they are tall like a rubber-plant. You can set your big specimens of Norfolk-Island-pine, philodendron, monstera, and others out of the light for as long as weeks at a time, but you have to get them back to full light to renew themselves if they are to be with you indefinitely.

The point is that plants need light for photosynthesis, the process of food manufacture in the leaves; denied this, they eventually die. Most flowering plants require sun for bloom—some more, some less. Wax begonias and impatiens (especially the newer hybrids) bud well in a fully light place; African-violets (in winter), azaleas, geraniums, poinsettias, and sweet-olive require sunshine. But you don't need to think in terms of exposures, as north or south, for a north window may be fully lighted and a southern one shaded by evergreens or a building. Just think in terms of what a plant will receive in a given location. And don't blindly follow those directions that come with florists' plants. If you put a full-bloom cyclamen in a sunny place and let it dry out between drinks its days will certainly be numbered. It needs full light to open its generous crop of buds—but full sun will fade the open blooms—and any dryness of soil will cause a fast demise.

2. GROW THEM COOL. Plants really don't have the exact temperature requirements you may have been led to believe. Furthermore, in every room there are cooler areas, as next the glass, and warmer places as on a plant stand set back a little from the windows. Many a plant will thrive at 50 degrees that dies at 70 degrees. If plants are grown in the living room, we hope they will be tolerant of our comfortable 72 to 75 degrees. Certainly the African-violet is, but don't count on the geranium. Anyway, it's usually cooler at windows and if you arrange your plants there and at night lower your thermostat from 75, say, to 65 degrees, *most* plants will thrive, even the tropicals. In the dining room, I turn off all but one radiator except in the coldest weather (for we eat mostly in the casement offset in the kitchen that faces the Look-Into Garden outside). Begonias, ferns, various gesneriads, and many vines enjoy the cool dining room.

In the Plant Room, I set the thermostat at 68 degrees for daytime. When the spring sunshine is strong, the temperature may go above 75 degrees, but the plants don't mind, for then I open the storm door a crack to let in a little fresh air. I lower heat to 60 degrees at night except in very cold weather. Then I know the plants next the long window, where there is no storm sash, will be trembling at 50 degrees or worse (even if the thermostat is set for 60), so I keep it at 68 degrees night and day and let nature tend to the night lowering. I also draw the venetian blind or slip cardboard between glass and plants on very cold nights.

In the Plant Room, *quite different kinds are accommodated at the same general temperature.* In the limited areas for plants that most houses offer, you could go mad trying to give your cyclamen the 50 to 60 degrees it prefers, your ferns 65 to 68 degrees, and your African-violets 70 to 72 degrees. In the Plant Room all these and many others live together in amity, for even here there is considerable variation in temperature. Just next the windows with no storm sash, it's cool enough for the cyclamen; on the room side of the plant trays, the ferns are comfortable; African-violets bloom at the west casements, which are protected in winter by extra glass sections.

3. CREATE MOISTURE IN THE AIR. In the average home that does not have a humidifying device attached to the heating unit or a cool-vapor

humidifier (plants dote on both), air moisture is best promoted by water-holding pebble-, gravel-, sand-, or vermiculite-filled trays. These can be of galvanized tin or iron made to fit plant stands or window sills and painted to match woodwork, or you can buy plastic trays, gray or green, in useful sizes. In the Plant Room, painted metal trays are inserted in the Formica shelf and set directly on the long radiator that runs underneath. The trays require a quantity of water about twice weekly to maintain a humidifying layer just *below* the surface on which pots rest. Bits of charcoal tucked among the stones keep the water sweet and unsmelly.

Under a fluorescent table fixture a green plastic 2- by 4-foot tray filled with pebbles provides an agreeably humid climate for the orchids and saintpaulias there. In both areas humidity of 45 to 70 per cent is maintained (*sometimes* 70 per cent plus in the cooler Plant Room), and this is about the best I can do. Of course, heat in the rooms must not go soaring, for humidity falls as heat rises.

When I read recommendations of a *steady* 70 per cent for certain plants, I shudder, for I know it can rarely be done here; I also have discovered to my surprise that many plants make do very well at 30 per cent. I run around with my hygrometer—an excellent instrument for checking both heat and humidity—and have been aghast at the low humidity rating. Then I observe that individual ferns in decorative pots and vines in suspended baskets are thriving despite the bad news. Of course, pebble-filled saucers can be placed under pot plants that aren't set on trays but then the effect is not so pleasing. Also, even without pebble trays, a *group* of plants will create fairly high humidity among themselves. Checking single plants in the dining room, I may get a reading of 32 per cent while the collection on the table will be enjoying 48 per cent.

Water-filled vases set among plants can also be a source of humidity as well as a means of propagation. I often place small bowls or pitchers of cuttings on the plant shelves. Fogging plants cleanses and refreshens them but it takes an awful lot of this applied moisture to increase humidity and, if it does, the effect doesn't last long. I spray my plants barely once a week except the orchids, which get frequent fogging. In the country plants don't collect dust as in the city, where daily fogging may be necessary to keep them clean.

If plants tend to yellowing leaves, it could be they need higher humidity. (It could be a variety of other ills, too, that we will think of later.) Anyway, I stopped yellowing on some *white* impatiens—the coral ones aren't so particular—with plastic-bag covers. I clipped two small holes in the plastic for ventilation and watered the plants as need indicated. To avoid bud drop on a gardenia, this is also a good if not beautiful practice. Apparently just when buds are about to open, there is need for higher humidity. If it isn't available, there is a sickening cannonade of those fat green buds. You could also shroud a whole collection of plants in plastic as some do, thus increasing humidity for a fluorescent cart of plants. In general, low humidity and overwatering are the most common cause of failure.

Now what to do about radiators? In the kitchen, vines on brackets hang some 3 feet above the radiator, and there they need a lot of water and frequent syringing at the sink if they are to prosper in that hot situation. However, with such attention, drying up of foliage and red-spider attacks are avoided, and in the eastern sunlight the vines fling out long streamers that in some years serve as curtains.

Radiators can be a real problem when you are locating plants. Usually the only sunny windows are above them. I have solved this in various ways. I used to spread a layer of air-conditioning filter on top of the radiators to prevent the sills above from getting too hot for the plants. Admittedly, this didn't contribute to human comfort, since it reduced the amount of heat flowing out into the room. It's really better to let the radiators alone and provide a low platform for plants set above them. A painted board or shelf raised on bricks or brackets will serve. Nicer-looking are footed lacquered Japanese trays. I set bright red ones above the end radiators in the Plant Room. They are a foot square and raise my big potted begonias 5 inches above the heat that flows harmlessly under them.

4. FRESHEN THE ATMOSPHERE. Plants need fresh as well as moist air. A close atmosphere is not conducive to health or bloom, and it can create all sorts of unpleasant conditions—leaf drop, yellowing foliage, fungus diseases. In most homes there is enough in-and-outing to admit fresh air through the casual opening of doors. If this air comes into rooms *adjoining* those where plants are growing, it's fine, for the air will be fresh but a little warmed before it gets to your plants. If you can't depend on this natural source of ventilation, occasionally open a window for a little while in a nearby room, and remember to close it before there is any chilling.

Plants do need a fresh atmosphere, but drafts and sudden cold will be obviously resented by loss of leaves. A Christmas poinsettia placed in your entrance hall for the festive season will be quickly denuded if it is subjected to cold from the frequently opened front door.

5. WATER SENSIBLY. Watering needn't be a problem but again it must be attended to regularly. Plants may go dormant if the soil is allowed to

dry out; then you can't get them going again until they take a rest that could be a matter of months. Or a fine crop of buds will blast if the soil loses too much moisture. Checking plants every day doesn't mean watering every day. If you have a great many plants, as I do, you soon thankfully discover that certain ones, especially in big pots, aren't going to need water more than every second or third day, or maybe only once a week. Remember, plants in plastic pots need less than those in clay where evaporation through the walls hastens drying out. Generally speaking, *all you have to do is to feel the soil.* If particles cling to your finger, the plant is *probably* moist enough for you to skip watering that day; if your finger stays clean from encounter with dry soil, water the plant—and thoroughly. Inevitably, there are exceptions to be noted later. Thus I keep cyclamens and ferns moist all the time but allow geraniums to get just a little dry.

How much water to apply? The whole soil mass should be moistened; avoid the little-and-often method. If your plants are on pebble trays, excess will run through onto the stones; if plants are in saucers, excess will drain there and you will want to empty the saucers soon after the watering, that is, if you are watering from the top. If you water from the bottom—either way is all right—plants will take a little while, but hardly more than an hour, to draw up what they need.

In any case, don't let pots stand in water very long. Standing water rots roots because it prevents aeration; oxygen does not pass through soggy soil, and standing water is the bane of a plant in a jardiniere. I put an inverted saucer or a block of wood under each plant in a jardiniere to make sure that plant roots aren't resting in a pool of water. Even so, frequent examination is necessary. (Recently I was horrified to find 2 inches of water under a fern; how could I have been so careless!)

Apply room-temperature or lukewarm, not cold, water. You can let water stand overnight, only I need so much this doesn't work very well. However, the one can of room-temperature water does suffice for the African-violets. If water is fit for you to drink, it's fit for your plants so don't worry over chlorination. If you have a water softener, draw water for your plants from the faucets *before* water enters the softener.

With big evergreen or shrubby plants—Norfolk-Island-pine, azalea, gardenia, hydrangea, palms—give a deep weekly soaking. Let the surface soil get just slightly dry. Then, if possible, set the pot in a pail or bowl of water and let it stay until the soil has drawn up enough water to feel damp, sometimes a matter of hours. This method insures moisture for the lowest roots that don't always get it with top watering alone.

Of course, all this is predicated on a proper soil mixture and proper potting. Those bits of crockery and the layer of roughage above the drainage holes prevent water from passing through too fast; they also provide a reliable exit. Heavy soil, holding moisture too long, is a death trap. The warmth of the room where plants are growing also affects the need for water. Plants grown cool require less than if grown warm. On sunny spring days, mine take gallons of water; in gray winter weather, it's a matter of quarts.

6. KEEP THEM CLEAN. Faded flowers, yellow or damaged leaves should always be removed. I keep a manicure scissors next the African-violets to facilitate this business, small pruners elsewhere for strong geranium stems or weak branches. My wax begonias shed a constant crop onto the pebble trays and these drying petals must be picked out. Rotting flowers or foliage near plants are a sure source of fungus infection, and that is something nobody cares to risk. Sometimes clay pots must be scrubbed as fertilizer salts discolor them. Of course, glass shelves must often be polished; if they feel sticky, find out whether aphids or scale haven't attacked the plants in residence there, and act accordingly, as suggested in Chapter 18.

7. LOOSEN THE TOPSOIL. In time, constant top watering compacts surface soil; it gets hard and cakes and prevents aeration of roots. In plastic pots there is no aeration from the sides and little enough from clay since air does not pass through moist soil. On that account air must penetrate from the top. A kitchen fork is a good tool for soil loosening. Operate gingerly; surface roots are damaged by deep gouging.

I thoroughly enjoy my houseplants even though I sometimes let enthusiasm run to too many. I hope you have fun with yours, too, and you will, with or without that ridiculously overrated green-thumb business if you check plants *daily* and manage these seven essentials:

1. Provide full light for the green growers, sun for the flower producers.
2. Keep temperatures on the cool side.
3. Try for a moist atmosphere.
4. Admit fresh air daily, indirectly in cold weather.
5. Water sensibly.
6. Keep pots and the growing area clean. Keep foliage clean.
7. Loosen topsoil so as to aerate the roots.

My plants, even when I do get beyond 100, require only a regular half hour six days a week, then one whole morning a week when I turn pots, rearrange, snip off faded flowers, train vines, prune a little, maybe spray with water, or with something stronger if there are signs of any undesirable visitors.

6

LIGHT IN THE DARKNESS

Setups and Culture with Fluorescents

It was a great day when some enterprising African-violet enthusiast placed plants under artificial light and discovered their marvelous response—continuous bloom regardless of weather and uniform growth with no weekly quarter turning. Today we know that practically any plant will perform handsomely under lights, especially flowering subjects—and those are the ones most of us want. What we must first determine is where to place the setups and which lamps or tubes to select—the familiar commercial type we install over stove, sink, or desk, or the "growth" lamps specificially manufactured for plants. Finally we must decide how close to the lights to place the plants and how many hours of illumination to give them, but these considerations are matters for experiment since conditions vary so from one home to another.

Types of Setups

Some gardeners enjoy extensive "light gardens" in a basement or unused room, perhaps a bedroom once the children have moved out. Large tiered fluorescent carts fitted with trays stand in many living rooms today. Then there are the table setups that light oblong plastic trays of plants or the round trays illuminated by circular tubes. Closets are sometimes fitted with lights and shelves to make a pretty little alcove garden.

In windowless areas, fluorescent lights make possible flowering-plant pictures like this. Here, in a corridor, a modern fixture is placed on an antique pine chest, the pink, lavender, and white African-violets a delight to all who pass by. On the right the timer and the hygrometer are great conveniences. George Taloumis photo

Designers of furniture are only just beginning to be aware of our need for *attractive* pieces whose primary purpose must still be the growing of plants; I hope these will soon be available.

Perhaps the greatest value of the fluorescent discovery lies in the opportunity it gives the apartment dweller with no bright windows or the homeowner whose windows are not light enough because of evergreen plantings or nearby walls that shut out the sun. Today really dark rooms do not preclude indoor gardening. Fluorescent lights can brighten any corner where you or the plants are. (I'm not going to talk about incandescents, which are too hot and not worth the bother, I think, of combining with today's adequate fluorescents.)

Very attractive are the light gardens set in bookcase shelves in a wall where books and ornaments are appropriate companions. Fixtures can be installed above the shelves and the interior painted white to serve as reflectors since these fixtures do not come with them. With bookcase setups, it is possible to have a variety of flowering plants in pleasant view right in your living room throughout the year. Not only African-violets but some of the other gesneriads, the smaller begonias, miniature geraniums (if it isn't too warm), and others look enchanting in these small shelf gardens.

In the kitchen, fluorescents fastened under cabinets and above counters provide a convenient place to grow culinary herbs in winter. Then there are the plant stands like my two-tube 12- by 24-inch Sylvania fixture with a reflector hood whose height can be regulated. Here I encourage "too quiet" plants to set buds and blooms; then when they are in full flower I move them to more decorative locations. However, the plant-stand garden, with pots on a pebble tray, is itself attractive. Filled with companionable orchids and saintpaulias or with African-violets alone, it gives pleasure to all who pass through the lighted but windowless passageway.

At the top of the west window of the Plant Room, I have a 12- by 48-inch glass shelf lighted by two 48-inch Natur-Escent tubes. For a decorative finish I had a wooden hood installed to conceal both lights and reflectors. However, unless you are willing to mount a two-step ladder at least every other day, and maybe daily, to check and water plants, you may find a high-up invention like mine inconvenient.

What Size Fluorescents

First of all, keep in mind that every square foot of growing area requires 15 to 20 watts of fluorescent light. Thus my plant shelf requires two 48-inch 40-watt tubes to illuminate the 12- by 48-inch space. Since the center areas of fluorescent tubes emit the most light (and you place your dark-leaved, rich-colored African-violets there, the pale pinks and whites at the ends), you want to get the longest possible tubes. But in the average home a 96-inch tube is a little too challenging. I prefer a pair of 48-inch tubes, set next each other for my high-up fixture, and, for the plant stand, two 24-inch tubes.

Growth lamps are more expensive than the older commercial tubes. Furthermore, experience has indicated that you can get fine bloom without special tubes and without incandescents. I've tried and liked various kinds of growth lamps—Gro-Lux in the plant stand, Natur-Escent now in the Plant Room—but cool whites (meaning they look cool), natural and daylight tubes are all satisfactory and are usually available locally. They cost about half what the growth lamps do. However, if you want peak performance from high-energy plants like geraniums that require the brilliance of summer days, you may want to install Sylvania's Wide Spectrum, Gro-Lux lamp with its inclusion of far-red energy.

Popular choices among conventional tubes are one daylight and one natural lamp. But with these two you will be providing a quantity of useless-to-plants yellow green components (upon which our vision depends) and less violet/blue and orange/red than plants require and the growth lamps supply. Among General Electric tubes, a reliable combination has been a warm white with a cool white or a daylight tube, and some people have liked Sylvania's Gro-Lux with cool white. Actually you can use the growth types alone or in any combination with standard tubes except with the Wide Spectrum lamps.

Here is a chart that shows what the different types of tubes supply.

Relative Qualities of Lights

Name of tube	Violet/blue needed by plants	Green/yellow not needed by plants	Orange/red needed by plants
Cool white	good	excellent	good
Daylight	excellent	very good	deficient
Warm white	deficient	good	very good
Natural	deficient	good	very good
Gro-Lux	excellent	deficient	excellent
Gro-Lux Wide Spectrum	excellent	some	excellent
Natur-Escent	excellent	good	excellent
Plant-Gro	excellent	good	excellent

Length of Life

When you put in new tubes, mark the date with a grease pencil. They do not last forever and a slowing up of growth and bloom is usually an indication that their power is waning—unless, of course, they are not aging but dirty, as can certainly happen in the city. There an accumulation of grime takes no time at all as well you know from dusting the furniture, so wipe off the tubes about once a month. Generally speaking, a year is about the outside limit for the usefulness of the growth tubes, and fifteen to eighteen months for the commercial types.

Under fluorescent lights on a shelf in a bookcase wall, the dwarf begonia 'Cleopatra' ('Maphil') perfects star-shaped brown-and-chartreuse leaves and airy sprays of pink flowers. Jack Roche photo

Loss of strength is particularly noticeable at first, then it decreases. If you compare the brilliance of new tubes with the light from some you have used, say, for one hundred hours on ten- and fourteen-hour stretches, you will readily see the difference. On that account, if you have adjustable fixtures, set the lights farther above the plants for the first week or two; then experiment with them somewhat nearer the plants.

Ideal Distances

It is quite impossible to say categorically at what distance from plants the light will be most beneficial or how many hours the lights should be on. Different plants react in different ways under different circumstances. In general, if foliage looks paler than it should or it seems to be reaching down, you can diagnose that the lights are too close for comfort. Variegation turning to all green might be another indication. On the other hand, if plants have a reaching look and budding is sparse, they probably should be placed closer and for longer periods.

With saintpaulias, claims are made for 3-inch distances as well as 10. When I tried 3 inches—and measurements are always made from the *top of the plant,* not the shelf—my plants appeared scorched; at 7 inches the standard plants prospered and the miniatures at 5. (These on the same shelf were elevated on inverted pots.) Preferred temperatures—cool for begonias, warmer for African-violets—are a factor, and we have all discovered that plants under lights need much more water and fertilizer than those growing in natural light. Anyway it's a good plan to start with growth lamps fairly high up, perhaps 12 inches above plants, commercial tubes, 10 inches above plants. Then, in a week, try lowering the lights.

As for hours of illumination, ten perhaps to start with, fourteen or even sixteen as experience indicates. If you have a timer—and I think they are just great—you can set it to go on and off for definite periods. If you don't have a timer, you will probably find it convenient to put your plants on your own get-up and go-to-bed schedule. Anyway, don't leave lights on all night except by accident, for all plants need a rest period—at least so I understand and consider only natural. I have heard a claim that they react well to constant illumination but that I'd have to observe with my own eyes.

In due course without great strain you will find out with a little experimenting what distance and what hours best suit the plants in your house. Just be sure to give them as regular attention under lights as at your windows and more food and water than your plants under natural light require.

The great advantage of lights comes with the tropical plants we want to keep in flower. Foliage subjects benefit less, but the variegated types like caladiums, coleus, red-margined dracaenas, and trailing velvet-plant do look especially fine. If you have room for them, you will be pleased with their performance. Of course, almost any plant benefits and nearly all can be grown together since most houseplants are daylight neutral and aren't particular about how much darkness (or lightness) they get. However, if long-night plants like the Thanksgiving and Christmas cactus and the poinsettias are grown in with, say, African-violets, and given the same light treatment, they won't produce flowers, only foliage.

7

A SCENTED INDOOR SEQUENCE

Fragrant Plants for Fall, Winter, and Spring

To the beauty of bloom a number of houseplants add the charm of fragrance. The scent of certain mature, heavily blossomed plants will actually pervade a room; when there are only a few flowers, you must bend to them to catch the sweet odor, except for the Paperwhite narcissus and the hard-to-grow gardenia. Just one open flower of these will do it. In the sixteenth century, Francis Bacon classified certain flowers as "fast of their smells," others as "free." The plants that produce flowers that are "free" are emphasized in this indoor fall-to-summer sequence.

Some of the most delicious of these need fairly cool conditions, night temperatures of 50 to 55 degrees. If you have a slightly heated, but never freezing, sun porch that would be a good place for Meyer lemon, "Maid of Orleans" jasmine, and sweet-olive. Or you could have a delightful cool and scented window garden of these and add a basket or bracket of white or dark purple "True Sweet" heliotrope. Be sure you are getting the fragrant kind; the big-flowered garden heliotrope is usually quite scentless. A south window *without a storm sash* will also usually be cool enough, and the cool-preference plants have prospered *next the glass* in my Plant Room where warm-preference plants thrive on the room side of the trays.

September–October On

CLERODENDRUMS. Cashmere Bouquet is one name for the big shrubby *Clerodendrum fragrans pleniflorum* that pours forth such a

Even one Paperwhite narcissus will scent a room. George C. Bradbury photo

strong fragrance from blush-white flowers from September into December if you can grow it fairly cool, around 60 degrees, and in full sun. (Grown warm, it does not bloom so long.) This plant will grow to 4 or 5 feet and is better for a large sunroom than for the average living room. Here is my 1963 note (before the Plant Room was built): "The clerondendrum would look fine if I didn't bump into it all the time and break the enormous leaves." If you attempt this one for its sweetness, keep pinching long growth back; this will reduce leaf size without affecting bloom clusters.

JASMINES. Poets jasmine, *Jasminum officinale grandiflorum,* is a shrubby vine with ferny foliage and rosy buds that open to white flowers of powerful fragrance, especially in the evening. In cool quarters, these appear intermittently from August through winter. Arabian jasmine, *J. sambac* 'Maid of Orleans,' also a shrubby grower, offers a profusion of small white flowers that fade through pink to maroon. This is perhaps the most fragrant of all jasmines; pinch tips to promote the budding that continues throughout the year in a *cool* place. Syringe frequently to avoid red-spider.

NIGHT-JASMINE, *Cestrum nocturnum,* has no daytime scent but in the evening the fragrance is powerful. Starry cream-white blooms open in repeated bursts throughout the year. A mighty shrub for cool growing, this one requires plenty of food and water and stern pruning to keep it house size. The fragrance suggests orange blossoms.

November–December On

SWEET-OLIVE. From Thanksgiving until June this shrubby evergreen, *Osmanthus fragrans,* opens a profusion of tiny creamy-white, sweetly fragrant flowers. I grow it at a south window without a storm sash where daytime heat hardly rises above 68 degrees and nights are about 55 degrees. Not a rapid grower, it hardly needs a shift oftener than every other year. Frequent syringing prevents pests and a summer in the garden insures profuse winter bloom. Sweet-olive is a charming companion for the lovely blue but scentless plumbago and the brilliant bouvardia.

FRENCH-ROMAN HYACINTHS AND PAPERWHITE NARCISSUS. One of the great pleasures of the indoor garden comes from these tender bulbs whose fragrant flowering can be scheduled to holiday and party occasions, Thanksgiving and Christmas, when I like to set up bright little still-life compositions at certain windows. At the end of Chapter 13 there is a schedule that I have relied on through the years to provide a procession of bloom from these two groups of choice bulbs.

BOUVARDIA. This delectably fragrant favorite for bridal bouquets is more often obtainable from a florist than by mail order. Choice in every way, *B. longifolia humboldtii,* shrubby and sprawling, opens tubular white flowers intermittently from Thanksgiving on to January. I grew it in a basket in a cool kitchen window but it really is too elegant for such quarters. 'Albatross' produces large flowers, 'White Joy' smaller ones but in greater quantity. 'Giant Pink' is a lovely coral shade that I particularly like, and these last two are cultivars of *B. ternifolia.*

January–June

GARDENIA. Not the easiest of houseplants, *Gardenia jasminoides* and the smaller *G. j. radicans* are more dependent on high humidity than most plants. They are among the most fragrant of our indoor subjects. Even one bloom will perfume a room. The gardenia requires full sun or fluorescent light. It is less likely to drop its fat buds if covered with a plastic bag with a few perforations, a device for health rather than beauty. Provide an acid growing medium or water occasionally with a solution of 1/2 teaspoon white vinegar to 1 quart of warm water.

CRAPE-JASMINE. Another so-called jasmine, the rarely grown *Ervatamia coronaria,* also known as Clavel-de-la-India, opens a long succession of handsome, 2-inch creped flowers from January through June. It thrives in a sunny location but blooms in the darkness of night. The fragrance is piercingly sweet. The shrubby plants need no pinching to develop into masses of shining green. The double form is known as butterfly-gardenia. Some winter this could be a nice stranger to introduce to your *cool* window garden.

CAROLINA-JESSAMINE. Golden-yellow, funnel-shaped flowers, more richly scented as the days lengthen, open through late winter on *Gelsemium sempervirens*. The plant may be quite motionless even through December, then it will start to grow and produce a lovely succession of bright flowers for some months. I like to train this twining evergreen on two crossed-wire arches.

MANY-FLOWERED JASMINE. This shrubby trailer, *Jasminum polyanthum,* blooms from the turn of the year as days lengthen and it goes on into summer. It is one of the most fragrant of all jasmines. A rampant grower with lacy foliage, this well-named, many-flowered jasmine soon needs a 6-inch pot and produces a mass of bloom on a strong support.

YESTERDAY, TODAY, AND TOMORROW. Sometimes called kiss-me-quick, *Brunfelsia calycina floribunda* has not been an unqualified success for me, but when I manage it properly, what a joy it is. Once I set a plant away in the cool "recovery room" when it wouldn't bud in the living room—probably too low humidity and too much heat there. It bloomed suddenly; one day it seemed all green, the next a profusion of lavender-blue trumpets fading to white and shaped like the flowering tobacco in the garden, the fragrance strongest at night. It grows to 3 feet and, if you have space for it and a cool spot, it will delight you from January to July.

Late January to Fall

YELLOWSTAR-JASMINE. Two of my favorite oriental vines are *Trachelospermum,* handsome and richly scented. Growing in the sunny west window of the Plant Room, the yellowstar-jasmine, *T. asiaticum,* starts to bloom late in January and is seldom without a little color even into fall. The white *T. jasminoides,* even more strongly perfumed, is in starry bloom from February through April, the yellow buds turning white as the days lengthen. If plants are placed under fluorescent lights in September, terminal clusters may open above glossy foliage even before Thanksgiving. I train this one around three or four plant stakes and maintain the same acid soil as for citrus and gardenia.

MADAGASCAR-JASMINE. Another favorite of brides is *Stephanotis floribunda,* the fragrant white waxen flowers having an Easter-lily scent. This vining plant may not bloom until spring but then it will continue until fall. I enjoy it now in the Plant Room and you too will discover that the stranger you have admired at the florist's can also be welcomed in your home. Even out of bloom, it is a handsome plant, happy at 60 to 70 degrees; when it starts to grow, the pace is terrific—inches a day. You can check the long stems by pinching them out. There will be some resentment but in due course the bare stems will become leafy. I have admired stephanotis for years. I find an April 2, 1964, note: "After weeks in bud, the stephanotis is opening white and fragrant. Rich soil and acid fertilizer like Miracid are beneficial and it looks nice trained on my favorite double arch."

LILY-OF-THE-VALLEY. For certain fragrance, and on twenty-one days' notice, there is nothing like the lily-of-the-valley. Cold-storage forcing pips or budded roots are not usually available by mail order until late December or early January, and your florist may not be able to get them for you before March or April. In any case, don't order until you are about ready to plant. Cold-storage forcing pips must not lie around.

These are the easiest of all fragrant plants to schedule and so delightful to have in bloom sentimentally for Valentine's Day. Timing them for this occasion, February 14, I plant a dozen pips about January 20, the roots trimmed back a third as directed. I like my 5-inch-deep, 6-inch-wide, rose-patterned Chinese bowl set on a black stand. I use pebbles, the same as for narcissus bulbs, but soil, peat moss, or other growing medium you may have on hand will do as well. Grown quite cool to the point of budding (pips blast if grown warm), they are then moved to a light but not sunny window. When I am energetic, I place the bowl in the cool garage at night to make those scented bells stay fresh for a long time.

Above, the white heliotrope, constant in flower and scent, but do watch out for white fly. *Below,* flowers of this evergreen sweet-olive are small but of marvelous fragrance, and bloom is constant through the year. Merry Gardens photos

The cream-white flowers of the night-jasmine, *Cestrum nocturnum,* are scentless by day but powerfully fragrant in the evening. Merry Gardens photo

March into Summer

CITRUS. In cool *extensive* quarters you can have orange, lemon, and grapefruit trees. One of the best of these for house culture in a cool area is Meyer lemon, *Citrus limonia* 'Meyeri.' Beauty, fruit, and fragrance recommend this tender shrub that starts blooming intermittently when quite small. Rosy blooms open to cupped white flowers that emit a fine lemony scent. Bushy or trained to tree form, it bears fruits of smaller size than *C. l. ponderosa,* which is also marvelously fragrant but a big awkward grower.

Move flowering citrus plants outdoors in summer and let the bees tend to pollination or manage it yourself indoors by touching each blossom with a small brush dipped in pollen. Assure acidity by watering frequently with a vinegar solution (1/2 teaspoon white vinegar to 1 quart of warm water), or if you are applying Miracid fertilizer to other specimens, as I do, give that to your citrus plants. Avoid scale that makes leaves sticky by spraying frequently at the kitchen sink.

GINGER-LILY. The ginger- or resurrection-lily, *Kaempferia rotunda,* brings the unusual to an indoor garden of familiar plants, and the tubers are easy enough to grow. The flowers look like great lavender-shaded violets and they have the exquisite perfume of lilies. Pot the dormant tubers from December to January for March-to-April blooms that emerge directly from the soil every other day or so for several weeks. Large patterned leaves follow flowering and make this a handsome foliage plant all summer.

AMAZON-LILY. The Amazon-lily, *Eucharis grandiflora,* is a jewel—and a challenge. I don't grow it every year but when I do I rejoice in my decision. The fragrant clusters look like white short-cupped narcissus with a touch of green. Flowers stay fresh for days and if I am lucky there are three successive bloomings, the one in midwinter most welcome of all. Do try this lovely thing. (Culture is given in Chapter 13.)

APOSTLE-PLANT AND WAX-PLANT. These two, like the Boston ladies' hats, are not something to buy but something you should have had. They require age to produce the growth and fragrance we all desire. My *Neomarica gracilis,* the walking- or house-iris or apostle-plant, is without doubt the most striking accent in the Plant Room, the great fans of leaves rising above the soil of the 4-inch pot and one 19-inch leaf dangling down with twin fans on the end. Fragrant purple irislike flowers appear in the midst of these, wedged in between the leaves late in winter, but to date there has not been what I'd call a crop. If the plant weren't so fascinating, I'd get rid of it, because I really want bloom, but it is indeed of unique growth. I don't cut off the suspended fans—though these are a fine source of more plants—but let them stay as I do offsets on the spider-plant. Either is well suited to a plant stand. For success with the apostle-plant, provide patience, a tight pot, full sun, and lots of water. I am told that leaf tips sometimes brown; my guess is that is due to inadequate moisture. Since I am inclined to overwater, the leaf tips on my plants stay green.

The wax-plants, both the big *Hoya carnosa* and the miniature *H. bella,* are darling basket or bracket plants but unless you inherit one you aren't going to get those honey-sweet flowers on a plant you buy for years—at least four, maybe ten! Meanwhile, the wax-plant is a handsome vine and how it grows from spring on. My young one has flung out a 3-foot tendril in about that many months; I fasten it to the window frame with Scotch tape. Warmth, rich soil, full sun, plenty of water when it's growing fast—again patience—are vital conditions.

8

AFRICAN-VIOLETS BLOOM AND BLOOM
Exploding the "Difficult" Myth

The great value of saintpaulias is the constant color they bring to window gardens as well as their decorative possibilities for centerpieces and coffee tables. It's true, they do pause briefly between periods of heavy budding, especially the large-flowered types, but they don't go dormant and, well treated, they offer a fairly steady procession of flowers throughout the year. I don't grow mine as a collection in basement or game room but enjoy them *on view* along with my many other indoor favorites on pebble trays in the Plant Room, as trailers on brackets fastened along window frames, on the broad sunny window sill in the living room, and also in front of a well-lighted north window in the dining room where they flourish with the indefatigable wax begonias. Small white African-violets highlight terrarium plantings.

African-violets are really easy, easy, and it's a mystery to me why everyone can't grow them successfully. Once when I was happily engaged unwrapping a new shipment—and how the good growers do protect plants so that never a leaf is broken in transit—a painter came into the kitchen. Like everyone else, seeing that it was plants I was unpacking, he put in his two cents' worth. "Lady, you got to be a doctor to grow them things!" His dire comment recalled a quite opposite remark made to me by a visitor at a Boston flower show. "My violets don't get any of those pests and diseases you write about. I never knew about them till I read your book." I gladly assured her that well-cared-for plants do stay

In a sunny east window between bookcases, African-violets thrive in winter on an iron bracket, on glass shelves, and on a pebble-filled metal tray with tall yellow marguerites for brightness at one end, and a purple heliotrope at the other for fragrance. Gottscho-Schleisner photo

healthy but that when you write a "complete" book, as I have done, you have to tell the whole grim story.

Of course you don't have to be a doctor to grow African-violets! In fact, my own experience has been so free of disaster that several years ago I didn't even recognize an attack of mite when it occurred on some porch plants during my absence through summer weeks of extreme heat. Anne Tinari made the diagnosis and sent me a bottle of remedial spray, but I followed my standard practice with ailing pot plants and pitched out the whole row, thus avoiding contamination with the healthy violets.

However, if mite should attack your own extensive collection, you won't want to discard it but will try to clean it up with a spray like Kelthane or with one of the granular insecticide systemics worked into the soil; either material also offers good control; many enthusiasts prefer the ounce-of-prevention technique and apply Kelthane once a month. Since I hang Shell Oil No-Pest Strips in the Plant Room, I seem to be able to avoid trouble indoors, without having to depend on spraying. (This is discussed further under "Trouble, What Is It?" Chapter 18.)

Light, Heat, and Humidity

African-violets are dependent on *regular* care, even more so, I think, than other houseplants. I never knew any plants to sulk as fast or as obviously as African-violets do when they aren't comfortable. Before the storm window was put up on the west side of the Plant Room, they complained vociferously to me, hugging the sides of the pots and literally screaming that they were cold. Of course, I heard them; I also fitted cut-out paper-plate supports under the foliage to help it straighten out again at the warmer window. In January when the light was poor, plants at one window made loud complaint, this time via elongated leaf stems and up-reaching leaves, for these plants are not shade-lovers indoors, as has been so mistakenly supposed. From October to early April they flourish *in full sun* in the Plant Room. To mitigate the glare in May before the Christmas-berry-tree leafs out, I set them back from the glass, letting the taller geraniums, sweet-olive, and other fragrant plants take the direct sun. In summer I provide full light, not dim locations, and move some plants to the screened porch where we can enjoy the flowers. However, when heat and humidity are extreme, I bring them back to the cooler indoors and there I continue to fertilize them.

Although they bloom well at windows, African-violets also prosper marvelously for me under fluorescent lights on one high-up shelf in the Plant Room and with warm-preference orchids under a table fixture. My policy is to move some plants, especially large-flowered types, to the lights as they complete a heavy period of bloom elsewhere. When the reliable heavy budders start again, I transfer them to decorative settings, preferably where I can look *down* upon the shapely pattern of leaves and the colorful bouquets of bloom. As for fluorescent culture, I do wish more attractive fixtures could be designed for growing under lights; now it is difficult to obtain a pleasing effect with light setups except under lights on shelves in bookcases or on kitchen counters.

One very agreeable aspect of African-violets is their preference for a room just about as warm as we like, around 70 to 75 degrees, even to 75 degrees. Like us, they can stand it somewhat cooler and don't mind it, briefly, a little warmer. Checking the thermometer in my Plant Room, I'm amazed at the wide variation plants endure there with equanimity. Sometimes the temperature drops to 60 degrees at night and then rises to 75 degrees or worse by day. This drop at night is certainly acceptable but not essential, as I used to believe, for plants in the living room where the thermostat is not set back in cold weather flourish without night coolness.

Saintpaulias do want a fresh atmosphere. Ever get a headache in a close room? From their reaction, I think they suffer the same way. Except on cold days, I "crack" the storm door an inch or so in midmorning and I leave it so for as long as weather permits. On warm spring and fall days I prop it open. In very cold weather, fresh air is admitted from the adjoining hallway.

African-violets delight in humidity. Most of my plants are set on pebble trays where the humidity regularly tests 65 to 70, *sometimes* to 80 per cent. Spreading over the trays, the saintpaulias look charming, a pink, lavender, and purple mosaic, and I compliment them every morning on my first glance as I come down the stairs. Kept filled with water right up to the base of the pots (but never with pots standing in water), pebble-filled trays provide a constant source of humidity, and little fogging and misting is required, except to keep plants free of dust. Plants grouped on the living-room window sill and used decoratively for centerpieces or placed separately on a coffee table are given a refreshing weekly spray at the kitchen sink—with warm water, of course—and always kept out of strong light and sun until foliage is dry to avoid spotting of leaves.

How to Water

Every day I *check* the plants, which doesn't mean I water them every day. However, they are so harmed by dryness, and the weather has such a variable effect, that it is important to go over them. Obviously, I don't feel the soil in every pot. You get to know that pots on the plant trays

African-violets need not be segregated. Here set back a little from the sun, they bloom continuously in the company of other plants. The white-edged plectranthus (which may go dormant) makes a pleasing accent, and the tall, shrubby, musk-scented iboza, blooming white in winter, is pruned to keep it below its 5-foot potential. George Taloumis photo

usually aren't going to need water more than every second or third day unless the sun is very strong. It's the separately potted African-violets in china jardineres or woven baskets that are less subject to scheduling. Of course, only warm water should be applied; cold water is harmful.

Most of my plants are in "squatty" plastic pots, adequate for such shallow root systems; a few thrive in nicely curved clay pots. For the mature plants on trays and the tiny rooting plants, top watering is indicated; for mature plants in clay pots with saucers, top or bottom watering, usually both. One thing about clay pots in saucers, it's easy to determine how much water is needed. If the saucer holds water after, say, half an hour, empty it; then water occasionally from the top to flush down fertilizer salts that otherwise may collect on pot rims or soil surface.

With clay pots you also have to take care that neither leaves nor leaf stems rest on pot rims where they are likely to rot. To avoid this, cover the rims with Leaf Protection Tape or foil.

Generally speaking, African-violets thrive with soil kept *barely* moist, not sopping wet, not bone dry. In dull weeks, take care not to overwater or overfeed. Most of the time I fertilize every time I water instead of the every two weeks or so recommended by manufacturers. I add only a "pinch" of plant food—that's less than quarter strength—every watering in sunny weather when plants can make use of the food. I find this gives better results than intermittent dosage. I prefer a plant food high in phosphorus like Peters 12-36-14, which leaves no residue on any foliage it may touch. However, it's probably wise to alternate fertilizers, say two or three a winter, since different ones have different values, especially as to trace elements. Hyponex, Liqua Vita, Miracle-Gro, Plant Marvel, Stim-u-plant, Black Magic are some of the brands I have used over the years. If you apply an organic fish fertilizer, which is excellent, don't let excess solution run into the pebble trays or the "flavor" will last much longer than you wish.

About Potting

One blessing of African-violets is their small root systems. You can grow even quite large plants for a long time in 2¼-inch pots, and 3-inch pots are about tops. To keep plants to a proper size for such small pots and in scale for my window garden, I frequently remove some of the large outer leaves. Of course, such plants are not being grown for exhibition; these should develop perfect whorls of leaves exactly placed. What I do to plants to promote bloom and reduce foliage might even be termed mutilation by exhibitors' standards. And great exhibition plants such as I see at the national conventions can be handsome indeed. However, to have a 2-foot spread of leaves, you must have somewhat more than a 2-foot area to devote to a single plant, and lots of us can't spare so much room.

Inevitably bare unsightly necks do develop if the big lower leaves are regularly removed. When plants get this look, I knock them from the pots and actually slice off enough of the roots for the plant to fit back into the same pot. I then set it low enough for the bare stalk to be covered with soil. (Frank Tinari tells me I ought to *spread,* not cut, the roots but the slicing doesn't seem to be harmful.)

Multiple crowns may also result in big plants though *modern* cultivars, except the miniatures and trailers, seem less prone to such growth. Thick growth constantly offers an invitation to separate the plants or to give them bigger quarters. This invitation I do not accept. I try to detect signs of multiple crowns early enough to pinch them off with tweezers without scarring plants. Furthermore, I have informed each and every plant that what I want is bloom, not a lot of fat foliage. I find it hastens bloom if very carefully I lift budding stalks above foliage when they are hiding underneath.

To promote shapely growth, plants are given a quarter turn once or twice a week, that is, the plants at windows. Those under lights mercifully do not require this turning, but they do need more food and water than the others, for they are exceedingly busy under those stimulating lights. You have to work out distances from lights and hours of exposure according to your own conditions. I place mature plants 7 to 8 inches from *top* of foliage to lights that are kept on 14 to 16 hours. Perhaps 8 to 12 inches will work better for you as for many others; you have to experiment a little. Small plants are set on inverted pots to bring them closer to the lights.

Soils and "Growing Mediums"

Since I live in the country and in an area to which nematodes have not yet found their way, I grow my African-violets in soil from the compost pile, which is all humus, sift it through a ½-inch screen, and lighten it with sand or perlite to make it open and porous. In the fall, I bring in a pail of this compost, screen it, and cover it with foil to keep in moisture. Then if repotting is necessary, I have soil at hand.

I have also grown African-violets in soils bought from African-violet growers and these have been excellent mixtures. If you live in an apartment, this source or one of the packaged soils available at hardware stores or garden centers will be a great convenience, although these usually need lightening with sand or perlite. Sand is not always available in small amounts but you can nearly always find perlite. With packaged soils, I start the liquid feedings at once at a fourth to a third the manufacturer's recommendation; for plants under lights I allow ¼ teaspoon Peters to 1 gallon of warm water.

The packaged materials are pest-free and weed-free. If you use your garden soil and it is not nematode-free (your County Agent can tell you), you will want to pasteurize it by baking but don't sterilize, which would destroy all the beneficial organisms. To pasteurize, fill almost full a large roasting pan that has a cover, with your own mixture of loam, peatmoss, manure, sand, whatever. Pour enough hot water over the mix-

Here African-violets take over the Plant Room, filling the pebble trays above the cabinets, blooming on the glass shelves in the south window. At the top of the west casements, they grow under lights. On the floor, a feathery jasmine covers a double wire arch, in the corner a cut-leaf philodendron rises from a gilt-papered container and vines trail down from the wicker baskets to complete the picture. George C. Bradbury photo

ture to moisten the whole mass. Put the cover on the pan, set the oven regulator at 180 degrees, and check with your meat thermometer. Do not count the time until the correct temperature has been reached. Then bake for about one hour. Don't turn the heat higher or bake any longer or you will overdo it, rendering the soil inert through excessive loss of nitrogen, which occurs under very high heat; 180 degrees insures a complete kill of harmful organisms, and this is your main purpose. This is a smelly but endurable procedure if you ventilate well. (I hear that covering the pan with one of the new bake-and-seal wraps and carefully following directions on vent holes avoids odor but I haven't experimented with this. It sounds like a good idea.)

After the baking, let the pasteurized mixture stand uncovered in a cool place for about two weeks. Stir it occasionally to insure thorough aeration. Then use or store it for future use in a covered can. Tightly covered, it won't dry out and be difficult to handle.

More Violets, Anyone?

It is no trick at all to increase or share your African-violet collection. You can always spare, preferably, a few firm medium-sized leaves rather than those from the last most mature circle of old leaves. But this whole process is discussed in Chapter 16 on propagation.

Hybridizers continue to offer new cultivars every year—deepening pinks almost to red, flushing whites with paler tones, bringing strong variations to foliage, a trend I can't say I like since I prefer foliage to set off the flowers rather than to compete with them. Personally, I dote on the "tender" lavenders like Tinari's 'Wisteria' and Fischer's 'April Showers' but then there are the reliable blush whites like 'Helen Van Zele' and the true pinks of 'Pink Philly' and 'Astro Pink.' 'Sophie' is a purple Rhapsodie with fine brilliance. Actually there are colors to suit every preference so we can each select according to taste; no lists are necessary.

Two trends you are sure to enjoy are the production of the trailers and of miniature African-violets. I do enjoy my "vining" African-violets, which are set on brackets. Be patient with the trailers, for they must reach a certain maturity before they send out those long shoots, maybe not till the second year. Miniatures grow in popularity and they are discussed in Chapter 12. You can have all the types and colors in these small editions, a boon to those with limited space. There is even a trailing miniature in the making.

Like the Boston lady, I wouldn't know much about insects and disease if I hadn't investigated most of them elsewhere. Except in dining room or kitchen, I hang a No-Pest Strip insecticide near the plants. You can't smell the lethal vapor that kills flying insects—other pests too, I notice, or else it prevents their development. Unless you are sleeping or eating in a room, I think this strip offers a perfectly safe procedure. With its protection, my African-violet plants indoors have had no pest afflictions. Yours won't either if you plant in nematode-free soil (naturally so or pasteurized), if you provide full light or winter sun, apply room-temperature water, and are careful about heat and ventilation. With such care, they are bound to thrive. Certainly you don't have to be a doctor to grow these plants. African-violets are EASY.

9

PANORAMA OF GERANIUMS

Their Infinite Variety

Geraniums, all on their own, constitute a beautiful—and fascinating—world of indoor plants. If you know only the standard reds and pinks that you see in window boxes and public parks, please read on, for I want to acquaint you with the many forms, colors, and scents of these paragons among houseplants which properly we should call *Pelargonium*.

The common or zonal geraniums (only they are really a distinguished group) can keep a cool sunny window gorgeously colorful from October to June provided *winter-blooming types* of mature size are selected and a few simple needs satisfied. Lately, it seems to me I've seen very few geraniums blooming in window gardens and I think the reason is that people expect the exuberant performance of their window-box and flower-bed geraniums, once they are potted, to continue to bloom just as fully indoors. And this won't happen. It is true that the zonals do not require a rest period nor do they have a dormant season unless your own cultural procedures force them to stop growing. And that's what you do when you cut back the ranging roots of outdoor plants to pot size and reduce tops accordingly. From these plants, even if grown in a cool sunny place, you are unlikely to get bloom before late February or early March.

Furthermore, what you bought for outdoor display were probably long-day varieties suited to hours of summer light and not the short-day plants that perform well on reduced winter exposures. Still left in their

genetic make-up, despite the hybridizer's minglings of complex strains in the interest of newer kinds with larger trusses, will be the factor of early bloom, and it's the early bloomers that make the best winter houseplants.

If you want geraniums for indoor color, go to a mail-order specialist who carries many interesting and unusual varieties. (If you have limited space, as who doesn't, you are sure to want some dwarfs and miniatures, and these are considered in Chapter 12, which is concerned with such "small treasures.") At one time I collected geraniums and filled all my sunny windows with them, both dwarf and standard varieties. I kept careful records of winter performance and noted that some of the very old and most enchanting and unusual geraniums, like the Rosebud varieties of 1870 and the Birds-Egg group from 1892, offered as much winter color here as it is claimed geraniums used to in our grandmothers' kitchens.

The Unusuals

You can have fun collecting these unusual geraniums, and you might like to specialize in certain categories. I've grown a great many of them with pleasure, for the different flower forms are fascinating.

'Apple Blossom' or 'Painted Lady' geraniums are rose, pink, or red, shading to white centers. 'Apple Blossom' itself is choice, a replica of the true apple blossom, and 'Souvenir de Mirande,' notably free-blooming in winter, and the vigorous 'Painted Lady' are also irresistible.

The 'Birds-Egg' geraniums are fairly rare today but single and double pink or white Birds-Egg can be found, also 'Mrs. J. J. Knight,' a free-flowering white to pale pink. A characteristic stippling, darker than the rest of the flower, and usually rose-red, appears on the petals, most often on the lower ones. Enchanting is the word for these Birds-Eggs.

The Carnation-flowered geraniums, not so rare, have distinctive serrated petals as if clipped with pinking shears. The Fiats are of this type

Geraniums occur in many forms. *Above left,* the single Birds-Egg geranium, *above right,* the double form, both charming and unusual, come pink or white with rose-stippled petals that give them their name. *Center left,* a white, cactus-flowered zonal, 'Noel'; *center right,* the variegated 'Miss Burdett Coutts' with purple-pink-splashed leaves and single vermilion flowers. *Below left,* the pretty 'Apple Blossom Rosebud' geranium blooms heavily through winter; *below right,* the handsome Lady Washington 'Salmon Splendor.' Merry Gardens photos and wonderfully reliable. I have long appreciated the bushy, light-pink, semidouble 'Enchantress Fiat,' the compact white-flushed salmon 'Princess Fiat,' and 'Mme. Thibaut' with a sharply cut picotee edge. You will find that the Fiats seem to require more water and fertilizer than most other geraniums.

The Cactus-flowered geraniums are mainly doubles with uneven twisted petals. 'Morning Star' has apricot blossoms, and 'Noel,' the white poinsettia of the group, is a fine winter bloomer as it should be considering its name.

Resembling the flowers of the garden perennial, the Phlox geraniums are singles with dark eyes. 'Ecstasy,' one of the loveliest of all singles, is cream-white with a pale coral center, and 'New Phlox' is white with a bright vermilion eye.

'New Life' geraniums are interestingly variable, particularly the single 'New Life' sometimes called 'Peppermint Stick.' One plant may bear an all-scarlet flower, along with a pink-centered white, and a third having stripes or flecks—amusing if not beautiful. 'Double New Life' is sometimes called 'Stars and Stripes.'

The Rosebuds have double flowers just like those of tiny rambler rosebuds before they have opened. 'Apple Blossom Rosebud,' the white flowers carmine-rimmed, has been prized for generations. It blooms well and the clusters always last a week for me. You will love it. There are also pink, red, and crimson Rosebuds. The memory of a whole window garden of them has stayed with me for years.

These are by no means all of the unusuals among the zonals; the narrow-petaled 'Fingered Flowers' ('Formosa'), a semi-double salmon, and 'Mr. Wren,' a single scarlet with white edges, are also interesting. I know I have run on about these special types—too long maybe—but I am eager for you to know what fascinating possibilities there are among them in case you have to date been acquainted only with the more typical zonals. You might start your acquaintance with one plant from each unusual class and what eye openers they will be.

Zonals in Winter

Standard zonal types include many excellent winter-flowering plants, among them the beautiful bright red 'Irene' and 'Salmon Irene,' as well as those like the white-eyed rose 'Genie,' the rose-pink 'Party Dress,' and scarlet 'Toyon' that do not usually carry the Irene name. Then there is the fully double 'Better Times,' a lovely crimson with a touch of white in the center. This is such a heavy winter bloomer that commercial growers sometimes complain about the incessant cleaning up their benches require.

Good whites are scarce, but 'Merry Gardens White' is fine for winter. All these and many more are starred in my winter records: 'Dreams,' 'Mrs. E. G. Hill,' 'Jeanne,' 'Lullaby,' 'Magnificent,' 'Shocking' (though it is enormous), 'Tangerine,' and my namesake, 'Helen Van Pelt Wilson,' a single lavender-pink with a white center. Generally speaking, put your trust in those the catalogues may describe as "free-flowering pot plants."

Fancy-leaved Geraniums

Brilliant foliage occurs on many of the zonals, and these are called Fancy-leaved or Colored-leaved geraniums. They are variously classified, Tricolors include 'Happy Thought' with gold, rust, and green leaves; 'Lady Cullum' with a red, brown, and green zone on a gold leaf; 'Mrs. Pollock,' another zoned gold leaf; 'Miss Burdett Coutts,' with a pink, brown, red, and white leaf; and my favorite, 'Skies of Italy,' with a dark green gold-edged leaf, splashed crimson and orange like a maple leaf.

I am also partial to the green-and-whites, such as 'Cherry Sundae,' 'Mrs. Parker,' and 'Silver Lining,' the gray-green leaves deeply splashed with white, the young foliage flushed pink. Among the bronze-and-gold types are 'Alpha' and 'Bronze Beauty.' 'Verona' has a bright pure gold leaf. If you want a fairly dwarf grower for a limited space, 'Sprite' offers pink-tinged green-and-white foliage, and 'Greengold Kleiner Liebling,' a green leaf irregularly margined in gold. 'Mme. Margot' (also known as 'L'Élégante' and 'Sunset') is a very pretty cream-bordered, pink-tinged ivy geranium with large lilac-white blooms, a charming bracket plant in or out of bloom.

The Fancy- or Colored-leaved geraniums require more care than the green-leaved zonals. In fact, the brighter the hues, the weaker the plant seems to be; yet it is those of strongest coloring that appeal most. The Fancy-leaveds require sunshine to bring out the strong variegation but not full sun in summer, rather morning sun with afternoon shade. It is the new growth that has the best color, so you want to keep this coming along with frequent pinching to induce branching. Although the Colored-leaved types generally have rather light root systems, they seem to require proportionately larger pots, and perfect drainage is essential. Use 4-, 5-, and eventually 6-inch pots for these, with a quarter of the pot filled with drainage material and above that soil that is not overly rich. Fertilize enough to keep growth coming along but not so much that foliage gets pale and lush—a nice balance to work out. Too much moisture or too much plant food reduces color.

If these geraniums come to you rather the worse for their journey (even more so than the others, and none is a good traveler), do not be alarmed, they will recover. Also, if the light is dim in winter, the silver-leaved and the tricolors may put out new leaves that are not flat but umbrella-shaped. At one window mine usually do this but when the sun gets around there in late winter, they give up the idea of being parasols.

The Scented-leaveds

This is an extensive group and the plants get to be enormous. Of course, geraniums really are shrubs. One winter I gave over the south living-room window to them and by spring we could hardly see out. However, these are endearing plants, the crushed leaves emitting scents of apple, lemon, lime, orange, rose, mint, and other odors. Among the more compact growers are the lemon 'Prince Rupert,' rose 'Lady Plymouth,' and orange 'Prince of Orange.' However, I always want the great rambling peppermint, *P. tomentosum,* so attractive in my black iron kettle, and *P. graveolens,* the old-fashioned rose geranium. This probably offers the most roselike scent, but this opinion is a matter of noses, I have found.

Ivy-leaved Geraniums

The varieties of *P. peltatum* are handsome trailers that are a joy even as green plants, for they don't burst into full bloom until about mid-February, continuing then into autumn. The glossy foliage does resemble English ivy but it is more brittle and it has a pleasant "green" odor, some say of cucumber. *Peltatum* means shield-shaped.

Usually there isn't room for more than one of these big basket plants so perhaps you will prefer, as I do, the lavender 'Barbary Coast' or 'Santa Paula,' or the deep purple 'Joseph Warren.' One of these will introduce a shade not seen in your zonals. Two excellent ivies of variegated foliage with lavender or pink flowers, variously called 'L'Élégante' and 'Duke of Edinburgh,' depending on where you buy them, also make excellent houseplants, with richly tinted foliage in full sun. And there is a miniature ivy, 'Gay Baby,' with lilac-white flowers and close-set leaves, a delightful novelty. In summer, the Ivy-leaveds will not endure long periods of high heat and humidity; they are most comfortable in full light with only a few hours of preferably morning sun.

Still More Temptations

Although they are ungeraniumlike in looks and behavior, you may be attracted to climbing and cactus types as I have certainly been. But I think they are an acquired taste like olives. The knotted storksbill, *P. gibbosum,* is a tuberous-rooted climber with fragrant greenish-yellow evening flowers in spring, nice gray-green leaves, and a corky stem. Following bloom, it sleeps deeply and must be put aside. The sweetheart geranium, *P. echinatum,* also tuberous rooted, is a cactus type with spring growth and flowers "lovely as an orchid," heart-shaped, white, and red-flecked. This blooms for a long period, sometimes continuing on my front steps into autumn.

I treat the Lady or Martha Washington or Regal geraniums (*P. domesticum*) as disposable pot plants, handsome for a four- to six-week spring display. They can be obtained from mail-order houses early in spring in 2½-inch pots but with full-sized buds and blooms. Most varieties cost less than a dollar and do a lot for the window garden at Easter time.

Culture

To get the bloom you want on geraniums, obtain, as I have said, good winter-flowering varieties and propagate these by cuttings of new growth. Taken May to June, and potted on, they will be of a size to bloom by October; August–September cuttings are unlikely to set buds before February. In Chapter 14 you will find directions for cuttings in general; here I'd like to point out that an easy-easy way with geraniums is to insert each cutting in a little pocket of sand, perlite, or unmilled sphagum in a 3-inch pot of standard geranium soil. New roots readily form in the sand and grow out into the soil. And you won't have to transplant.

Pot geraniums in a half and half mixture of good garden loam or compost and sand or perlite and apply a liquid fertilizer low in nitrogen. The old idea of poor soil kept dry is no good. If you are collecting, you may want to prepare a special *Pelargonium* mix:

3 parts garden loam
1 part leafmold or humus or peatmoss
2 parts builder's sand or perlite (this increased if garden loam is stiff and clayey)
5-inch potful of low-nitrogen fertilizer for each bushel of the above or 1 teaspoon for each 5-inch pot

Make sure drainage is adequate and that roots of standard blooming-size plants have at least a 4-inch pot. Geraniums should never be actually rootbound. As for watering, let soil "approach dryness" but never really dry out before you water. Then be thorough so that the whole root ball is moistened.

Full light, preferably a flood of sunshine, all a bright south or east window will afford, is the first requisite for success; next, a somewhat cool location. Even at 45 degrees, geraniums will bloom a little, but somewhat below 68 degrees is preferred by day with temperatures dropping about ten degrees at night. In my very sunny Plant Room with south and west exposures, I usually set the thermostat at 60 degrees at night.

Only moderate humidity is necessary, 40 to 50 per cent. In fact, high humidity may be resented as it sometimes is here in July when heat and humidity soar and the potted porch plants droop. The ivy-leaveds particularly want fairly dry air and are well suited to the conditions of the average home provided they are not overwatered. Don't crowd plants at the window, and do turn them frequently to keep them shapely. They need space to develop evenly and benefit from a good circulation of air around them.

If, despite your good care, your geraniums in winter look sickly, if growth is lank and soft instead of fresh and crisp, if the flowers are not well formed and too few, check over these essentials of health for geraniums. Briefly they are sun, coolness, some humidity, sensible watering, adequate pots, space to develop, and a fresh atmosphere.

10

BEGONIAS—THEY NEVER FAIL

Carefree Plants for Light or Sunny Places

Begonias are indispensable, perhaps the best of all winter-flowering houseplants, especially the undemanding wax type that thrives and blooms indoors at any light window or accepts the winter sunshine as you please. I use these single and double well-named everbloomers, *B. semperflorens,* as indoor "bedding" plants. In pots of different sizes and little tubs they thrive among green plants at a northern exposure or on the room side of the long plant tray in the south window of the Plant Room. In either location they bloom all year long, for I keep a few in the Plant Room through summer to avoid a stark look there after the other plants have been moved to the porch.

Wax Begonias

You can pick up wax begonias with single or rosebud (double) blooms at roadside nurseries, selecting lovely unnamed varieties, or you can be more definite from a mail-order house. Many varieties are offered and at moderate cost. I like the Geneva series of doubles in pink and white. In the Cinderella series are charming singles with bright little yellow tufts of bloom in the centers—all these with green leaves. I don't care for the red-leaved varieties.

About all you have to do for any of these semperflorens—aside from routine care—is to gather up the daily cast of flowers and occasionally pinch back some of the exuberant growth to keep plants shapely, but let some stems grow longer for a pendant effect. If plants get leggy by spring and you want them for next year, simply cut them back hard, to 1 to 2 inches, and give them a summer outdoors. If you don't want to carry them over, plant them directly in a garden bed where they will bloom all summer once they grow up after the pruning.

Indoors, take care not to overwater, for their succulent growth seems to invite soaking; I keep the soil in my plants just nicely moist as I do African-violets and find that the 5-inch tubs take quite a lot of water. Rarely do pest or disease trouble a wax begonia. In fact, though there are certainly more spectacular flowering indoor plants, not one is more regularly dependable; if you live in an apartment, you should cling to them. And once you acquire plants they are yours for good since 5- to 6-inch cuttings taken any time of year will soon root in a vase of water.

The calla-lily begonias are a type of semperflorens but they are certainly too finicky for me. I gave them up years ago but I still react enviously when I see them flourishing in a friend's greenhouse. If you have the patience to cope with them, you will find these really pretty plants rewarding. They require full light, protection from drafts, and very little fertilizer until pots are root-filled. My friend Elda Haring, who is successful with the callas (and all begonias for that matter), recommends a light soil mix—two parts loam, one part peat, and one part sand. She advises growing them quite dry in winter with just enough water to keep leaves crisp; even when they are in active growth in summer, care must be taken not to overwater.

Angel-wings and Stars

The wax begonias are but a small part of the story. Many large, almost treelike kinds produce in winter and spring handsome panicles of pink, white, or red bloom. Then there are some delightful trailing kinds. If you consult the catalogue of a specialist, you could be overwhelmed, for great is the selection, so here are suggestions for some of the never-fail plants with interesting leaf forms that my friends and I have enjoyed.

My first choice among the big ones is certainly the angel-wing 'Corallina de Lucerna,' whose great pendant pink clusters come wrapped in cellophane. The dark green, white-dotted pointed leaves do suggest wings, angel or otherwise. I have only the complaint of exuberance, for it

Above left, the smooth leaves of the Rex begonia 'Merry Christmas' are brilliantly zoned from dark red centers through pink and green and pale green areas to a purple-red edging. *Above right,* the trailing *Begonia scandens,* whose feathery white flowers have a delicate air, are a pleasant contrast to window vines of more stalwart appearance. Walter Haring photos. *Below left,* the leopard begonia, so called for its yellow-spotted foliage, is a sturdy grower with clouds of pink flowers; *below right,* a star begonia, *Begonia* x *sunderbruchii,* with emphatic dark green leaves supports strong stems of larger individual pink-white blooms. Merry Gardens photos

is difficult to keep this cane type to what I think of as room size of 4 feet or so. To insure 'Corallina's' limited but continuous presence, I have worked out an ingenious year-by-year exchange with a neighbor, Irving

Sabo. He has an enormous Plant Room and nothing grows too big for it. So at the end of summer my great begonia goes to him, and to me a manageable 18-inch specimen is presented in the fall, this started by Irving from a rooted cutting of the year before. At the west dining-room window on a lacquered Japanese tray, 'Corallina de Lucerna' is a lovely sight with the brook and cliff seen through the glass for background.

Among lower-growing angel-wings are 'Orange Rubra' and pink 'Pinafore' and the lovely 'Lulu Bower' with faintly spotted leaves and gorgeous coral flowers. Then there is a large group of compact canes and angel-wings, notably the Belva Kusler hybrids, well suited to limited living areas. Of these three are well worth considering: 'Clara Elizabeth' with huge clusters of white flowers and tightly packed dark green leaves, 'Gwen Lowell' with tall clusters of white flowers and bronze foliage, and the low-spreading 'Lenore Olivier,' the flowers a sparkling red, the leaves coppery.

In the shrublike group is a particularly good winter bloomer, *B. scharffii,* with round bronzy leaves and pink blossoms that look like purses dangling from the arching stems. 'Thurstonii' is a rugged old favorite with handsome rose-pink flowers in spring and summer and glossy cupped metallic leaves. The hybrid, *B. digswelliana,* offers a different form, low and spreading; it blooms over a long period through winter, with pendant clusters of pink-to-red flowers and small shining dark green leaves.

In the rhizomatous group with thickened stems are two large handsome, somewhat procumbent growers, beautiful in pots or baskets. These have long borne the onus of "beefsteak" begonias, but I have never seen the likeness. They carry their pink sprays high above the foliage and delight me from January to July. Now more appropriately called the pond-lily begonia, *B.* x *erythrophylla* (*B. feastii*) has round leaves, rosy shaded beneath, and *B. e. helix* is a pleasing ruffled form. The heavy stems reach beyond the pot rim, making these two particularly good shelf plants. The lettuce-leaf B. 'bunchii' has charming curled and crested leaves.

The foliage of the pink-flowering star begonia, *B. sunderbruchii,* is striking, bronze-green and silver-banded. Spectacular is the word for the yellow-spotted leopard begonia with the fearsome name of *B. manicata* 'Aureomaculata,' but don't be put off, for it is a beauty with flowers in tall airy panicles. Also for interesting foliage are *B. masoniana,* the Iron Cross begonia, and its cultivar 'Tricolor,' the brilliant leaves likewise boldly marked with a darker cross. These bloom late winter into summer.

Rex Types

The Rex begonias are exotic foliage types, with dramatic leaf contrasts and colors. In winter they may rest somewhat and lose some of the larger leaves, but they do not go dormant, as is often supposed. New growth appears in spring, when plants should be put in fresh soil. Among the many attractive cultivars are 'Curly Silver Sweet,' the ruffled leaf silvery above, pink underneath; 'Helen Teupel,' the deeply lobed leaves purple-centered and patterned silver and rose; and 'Merry Christmas,' the zones of the smooth leaves well defined, the centers red, surrounded by a silver-and-pink area, the outer zone pale green, the edging purple-red—sounds like a stormy sunset. It would be easy to get caught up in the Rex begonias to the exclusion of others in this diversified family, for there are also the Rex miniatures to consider.

Trailing Begonias and Others

At least three trailers are well known to me. 'Ivy Ever,' one pictured in my tray collection, has pointed, green, red-veined leaves and pink clustered blooms. Limminghei is a winter charmer with salmon blooms and a graceful habit for shelf or basket. Feathery clusters of long white flowers and small glossy crinkled leaves make *B. scandens* a treasure. The trailing begonias have a delicate air among the heavier vines at my windows, and I do not entrust their brittle stems to outdoor breezes or summer heat.

The handsome summer begonias are tuberous rooted, glamorous for outdoor hanging baskets. I am told that if you have accommodation for it under lights indoors, you can keep a hanging basket plant in bloom for two or three months longer—a beautiful prospect.

Recently I have seen at flower shows, but not yet grown, something quite new, the Rieger-Elatior begonias from Germany. In this country they will be introduced by Mikkelsen, Inc., from whom have come our lovely new poinsettias. The Rieger-Elatiors, singles and doubles, with larger blooms than wax begonias, are crosses between the winter-flowering *B. socotrana* and the tuberous summer types. Apparently they bloom through most of the year. They look grand and you will probably want to try them as I shall.

The Christmas begonias are handsome gift plants, especially the two pinks, 'Marjorie Gibbs' known as Bizzie Lizzie, and 'Lady Mac.' These

Small specimens of seven favorite begonias are set in plastic trays filled with pebbles. *In the left tray, back, Begonia masoniana,* called Iron Cross, and the trailing *B. scandens; center,* the ferny *B. foliosa, and in front, B. limminghei. In the right tray,* the dwarf Rex 'It' *at the back,* 'Ivy Ever' *in the center,* and *B. erythrophylla helix,* a ruffled form of the familiar pond-lily or beefsteak begonia. Charles Marden Fitch photo

require a quantity of water and deep soaking weekly, the same as the shrubby azalea. If you receive one at holiday time, grow it on till it begins to go dormant and is no longer attractive. Then I'd say discard it unless you want to take the same trouble with it that you may for a cyclamen, as described in Chapter 14.

One autumn, for new and old acquaintance' sake, I ordered seven specimen begonia plants to enjoy first on the narrow window shelves and, as they prospered, on a table in two 8- by 10-inch plastic pebble-filled trays that you see in the photograph. So I disclosed the fern-leaf *B. foliosa,* a thin-foliaged plant, and 'It,' a pretty Rex oddity with small silver-spotted leaves, one of the many dwarf types so useful if you haven't room for the big ones. Another year, always on the lookout for

At Christmas time, I like to bring out my madonnas and place them in a setting, as here, on the hall console below the gilt mirror, with the vining *Begonia scandens* for a graceful compliment. George C. Bradbury photo fragrant flowers, I grew 'odorata alba' but I was disappointed, for it was certainly not "odorata" here. This species was the first begonia introduced into cultivation from Jamaica to England in 1777.

Perhaps you would like to collect some miniature and dwarf begonias of which there are many delightful and tempting varieties. In Chapter 12 on "Small Treasures" these are described.

Culture

As for growing needs, I pot my begonias in light, porous soil, half pure sifted humus from the compost pile and half sand or perlite with *assured* drainage in the pots, for these succulent plants will not tolerate wetness. On this account, I like to set plants in the pots with a barely rising crown rather than a depression where water might collect. Without an easy source of compost, you could depend on a packaged potting soil, or on Jiffy-Mix or Redi-Earth, and add one third part of perlite to either for drainage. Then there is a popular soilless mix that consists of 3 quarts peatmoss, 3 quarts vermiculite, and 3 quarts perlite with 2 teaspoons of ground limestone.

Along with the other houseplants, my begonias thrive in a 60- to 70-degree temperature and enjoy the up to 70 per cent humidity of the Plant Room. However, they do not require it, for they also bloom well in living rooms that are not nearly so humid, except the trailers, which seem to need the higher humidity.

Grown with adequate humidity and not too warm, begonias are rarely troubled with pests. They have not troubled my plants. However, aphids might appear and crinkled leaves and stickiness would be the indication, and there are reports of mealy bug and white fly. An aerosol bomb containing non-toxic pyrethrum-rotenone is effective against all these pests. More likely begonias fail from overwatering, which causes plants to rot at the soil line. But that is easily avoided for these beautiful and essentially carefree houseplants.

11

VINES ARE MY DELIGHT
Grace for the Window Garden

The vining plants have long been my delight and I can never resist adding more of them. The trailers, the climbers, even the sprawlers bring a lively grace to the Plant Room and to windows elsewhere that may have no other plants. And most vines move right along; you know they are really growing, and when they are fast, it's fun to measure them. Furthermore, well-grown and properly placed vines are wonderfully decorative whether framing a window alone or making a frame there for a window sill or tray of upright houseplants below. Lamium has even served me as kitchen curtains, much less trouble than up-and-down starched white ones.

Vines are the blending plants; they harmonize disparate groupings or individually adorn choice wicker or metal baskets, old and new oil-lamp brackets, shelves, and window ledges. Unusual containers become them. In the course of my travels I have collected for them, among other oddities, a copper soft-soap holder in Amsterdam, tin baking dishes in Albuquerque, and high brass trivets in England that nicely elevate small prostrate growers set among pot plants on the broad window sill in the living room.

Green, Tinted, and Variegated

Many vines are vigorous enough for almost any exposure. If you are

In the sunny east window off the kitchen, sprenger asparagus graces one side of a double iron bracket; from the other, a grape-ivy flings out long arms of growth. The familiar philodendron in a brass birdcage container flourishes even in the subdued light of a north window. *Home Garden* photo

not one to hover over plants but enjoy greenery indoors in winter, some of the more unexacting vines are for you. For instance, there's the indestructible grape-ivy, *Cissus rhombifolia;* it has stood by me for years. The kangaroo-vines, *C. antarctica* and *C. a. minima,* are not quite so carefree but certainly not difficult, and the variegated forms are pleasing.

Although hardly unusual, I always want at least one philodendron. Familiar is the heart-leaved *Philodendron scandens,* often sold as *P. cordatum,* which has much larger leaves. You can pick up a plant of this in almost any supermarket and enjoy it even in a somewhat dim place; *P. panduraeforme,* a curiously lobed type called the fiddleleaf philodendron, and the deeply cut *P. squamifera* are both decorative and happy on a moisture-retentive log or totem.

Ivies—True and False

The true ivies could make a collector of you and are just the plants to bring variety of leaf form and coloring to an otherwise green window. Aside from a vaseful of sprays of the hardy green English ivy cut from the garden in August, I have shelf plants of the small-leaved branching types —*Hedera helix* 'Goldheart,' 'Merion Beauty,' and 'Sinclair Silver Leaf' —and the bushy, larger-leaved 'Maple Queen.' The ivies need fairly cool quarters; in a hot living room they tend to dry up or be covered with aphids. Weekly dousing at the sink or daily misting from a sprayer, also plenty of fresh air, will keep them in health.

Many green vines are called ivies. *Senecio mikanoides* is known as German-ivy; the small, light green leaves make it a pretty plant. It was one of my very first plants and is cherished accordingly, for it grew despite a child's fantastic cultural attention. The variegated Swedish-ivy is a little round-leaved vine, *Plectranthus oertendahlii* 'Variegatus' with striking white markings if it is grown in full sun and delightful pink-tinted flowers in spring. The all-green, white-flowered *P. nummularius* is also nice to have. I discovered these only a few years ago and now I wouldn't part with either of them or with the upright white-edged miniature that grows in my bubble garden. All are easy to share, since pieces root readily in water.

Inch-plants, *Tradescantia,* of many kinds have been enjoyed here. Green, tinted, or variegated, these small-leaved vines grow and grow, and you can root pieces in water for your friends or add them to a house bouquet. *T. blossfeldiana,* tinted purple underneath, grew madly in my kitchen and will grace yours too even if you set it back from the light. It readily produces purple flowers but they are hardly special. The white inch-plant, *T. albiflora* 'Albo-vittata,' is handsome indeed, an excellent contrast among green growers. To get strong variation, give this one sunlight. The highly colored, striped zebrinas, sometimes called Wandering Jew, are closely related to tradescantia.

I also like two of the trailing peperomias but wish they weren't so slow. However, both *Peperomia fosteriana* and *P. scandens variegatus* 'Royal Gold' have been long-time residents. The purple-tinted velvet-plant *Gynura sarmentosa,* a procumbent grower, makes an excellent window-garden accent elevated on a brass trivet or an inverted flower pot, with pink wax begonias on each side. The 'Trailing Queen' coleus, carmine marking its green, is a bright performer in the sun. An apparently undiscovered vine that I prize is one I call goldvein; *Peristrophe angustifolia* 'Aureo-variegata' is its correct name. A crop of pretty little rose-purple trumpets decorate it much of the time but it is the pointed, yellow-streaked leaves that make it so delightful. It graces an also pointed ceramic container suspended by the dining-room window in winter, a corner of the porch in summer.

Flowering Trailers

Of the flowering vines, the ivy geraniums in pink, purple, and white are colorful from February through summer. If you like oddities, there is the trailing coriander geranium, *Pelargonium* x *coriandrifolium,* with tiny, lavender-to-white flowers and ferny foliage that looks like a refined parsley. I grew it on a bracket at the west casement. The samphire-leaved *P. crithmifolium* with huge clusters of pink-striped white flowers is a handsome trailer in bloom, peculiarly unsightly when resting but so interesting, and a climber, not a trailer.

I also enjoy such trailing begonias as the pink-flowered 'Ivy Ever,' salmon-pink *B. limminghei,* and the feathery white *B. scandens.* The vining velvet-plant *Ruellia makoyana* with silver-lined leaves offers tubular carmine flowers from fall into summer, a continuous pageant under lights or without at a west window, not demanding sun for budding. And now we are getting African-violets that trail once they reach maturity but they are not for the long reach like these other trailers.

I had such a lovely scented winter the year I emphasized the fragrant jasmines in the Plant Room. From August through most of the winter the ferny *Jasminum officinale grandiflorum* opens highly perfumed white flowers, rose-tinted in bud. The lacy, fast-growing *J. polyanthum* blooms freely and fragrantly with tiny pink-tinted white flowers from mid-January through February. The Madagascar-jasmine, *Stephanotis floribunda,* with waxen white, scented blooms, has been lovely for me late in spring in an east window. The star- or Confederate-jasmine, *Trachelospermum jasminoides,* with dark leathery foliage offers richly perfumed white stars from February through April. This one is better trained up than trailing down, so too the yellow star-jasmine, *T. asiaticum,* but I have already held forth on these favorites in Chapter 7.

The miniature wax-plant, *Hoya bella,* which makes such a pretty basket plant, and *H. carnosa,* which will grow to 20 feet and can be trained to frame a window, are charming vines and sweetly fragrant in bloom. You could even make a collection of hoyas, for catalogues list a number. One specialist claims three blooming periods a year with a rest period at 50 degrees from November to January.

Above, single or double brass or black iron brackets, like this, come from the hardware store and offer one of the most practical and attractive ways to grow plants indoors. *On the left* is the rabbits-foot fern, *Davallia fejeensis, on the right,* the trailing *Begonia scandens. Below left,* the trailing velvet-plant, *Ruellia makoyana,* blooms fall to summer in a west window, the little rosy-purple trumpets set off by the soft dark silver-veined leaves. *Home Garden* photos. *Below right,* the green-and-white *Peperomia scandens variegata* looks nice in a white ceramic basket suspended at a north window. George Taloumis photo

For most of us the difficulty with wax-plants is holding on to admittedly nice green vines but expecting bloom that isn't likely until plants are considerably mature, say four years old. Then, in rich soil in a sunny window, there will usually be a fine display every year from March into summer. Should your plants reach this stage, take care to guard the spurs which are the source of more flowers. Cut these off and the next year you will not get the scented waxen stars that you have patiently waited for.

In some years I have enjoyed the lovely azure *Plumbago capensis,* called blue-cape, which is such a charmer outdoors in California gardens and lovely blooming indoors here in October and November and again from January to April. This is a vine that requires a strong support, and it must be regularly pruned and thinned to room size early in September while it is still outdoors. The difficulty is control, for it requires an 8-inch pot in a few years and how many plants of this size can we include in our indoor gardens?

A delectable companion is a pink or white bouvardia, the white with a fine scent and a sprawler that must be staked, or trained as I prefer it, to a double arch. I form the arch with two 6-foot pieces of heavy ⅛-inch wire, bent at the halfway point. Bouvardia, the "flores de San Juan" of Mexico, is always lovely by Thanksgiving and continuously so into spring, especially the cultivars 'White Jo' and 'Albatross.' After the final blooming, bouvardias are discarded or new plants started from cuttings; they are not a good holdover. In the Plant Room I have also enjoyed bouvardia in a setting of blue-sage, *Eranthemum nervosum,* and the shrubby rose-red *Rondeletia odorata*—a pretty companion for many weeks though not fragrant here as the name implies.

The sun-loving passion-flower, *Passiflora* x *alato-caerulea,* a free-blooming hybrid in small size, has just come to my indoor garden and I admire its fast growth with 6 feet the goal. If I am successful, this will be a real indoor beauty for April, pink petals, a fringed crown of purple, white, and blue, and fragrant. The species *P. caerulea* is a more generous bloomer but for indoor gardening the cross is considered a better choice, and its flowers are among the largest and showiest of the many species and hybrids.

Trailing Gesneriads

African-violet enthusiasts have made these saintpaulia relatives popu-

The Christmas picture in the living room is bright with holiday gift plants—cyclamen, poinsettia, and kalanchoe—and bowls of white narcissus, forced for the season, all in a green setting of small-leaved ivy, trained on a wire arch, a begonia trailing down from the latch strip, and holly and rabbits-foot ferns on the window sill (George C. Bradbury photo).

Plants decorate every room in the house. A corner of the Plant Room in spring (*above left,* Walter Haring photo); in the kitchen, red geraniums and yellow marigolds in Mexican tin pudding dishes (*above right,* Peter Krieg photo). The dining room with grape-ivy in brass bird cages, a dried arrangement on the table in between (*below left,* Walter Haring photo); the south living room filled with African-violets in many colors, white impatiens, and an evergreen carissa for background (*below right,* Charles Marden Fitch photo).

Favorite houseplants include hypocyrta (above left, Peter Krieg photo), the balcony-type petunia 'White Cascade,' rescued from the garden in fall (above right, Walter Haring photo), and the ivy geranium 'Charles Turner' (below right, Wilson Bros. photo).

Two begonias: 'Iron Cross' and 'Lenore Olivier' (Walter Haring photos); zonal geraniums in a black iron kettle (Charles Marden Fitch photo).

Above left, the variegated vining wax-plant and the striped chlorophytum plant are pleasing companions suspended against a plain wall. George Taloumis photo. *Above right,* the passion-flower makes a dramatic April accent. Geo. W. Parks Co. photo. *Below right,* this trailing coriander geranium has ferny foliage and tiny lavender-to-white flowers, a fascinating and different vining plant. Merry Gardens photo. *Below right,* the unfamiliar vining goldvein, *Peristrophe angustifolia,* is choice with yellow-streaked leaves and little rose-purple trumpets of bloom. Alfred Byrd Graf photo lar, for they bring strong pendant growth to an otherwise flat pot-plant picture and also add enlivening yellow and orange tones. Of the various gesneriads I have grown, other than the saintpaulias, I prefer the strong vining types, and I must admit that few of these have ever put my eye out with a *great* crop of colorful bloom. I have seen such exuberance only on greenhouse plants.

The lipstick vine, *Aeschynanthus* 'Black Pagoda,' the goldfish-plant, *Columnea* 'Yellow Dragon,' the peacock-plant, *Episcia* 'Yellow Topaz,' and both *Hypocyrta radicans* with orange pouch flowers and *H. wetsteinii* with long-lasting red-and-yellow blooms along yards of green leaves have been attractive here, the last named and 'Yellow Dragon' the best bloomers I have had. And I liked *Nemanthus* 'Stoplight.' (Here I must mention *Nautilocalyx forgettii,* though it is upright, for its unbelievable name that I thought must be a joke.) Pots are set on brackets or in ceramic baskets so plants can hang down at the sides of window gardens in two rooms. Of course, like other trailers, gesneriads can be planted directly in hanging baskets lined with sheet moss gathered in the woods or bought from a florist-supply house. However, with such arrangements you are likely to have a drip problem and the planting itself is more bother than simple potting.

Exciting was one winter's trial of two Italian bellflowers, the white *Campanula isophylla alba* and the variety *mayii* with larger blue flowers. They bloomed off and on but were best from August to November and so not valued for the indoor garden, although as green plants they were lovely on brackets. However, they had a "drunkard's thirst," and the slightest dryness resulted in browning of the tiny leaves.

From the Garden—Nasturtiums and Petunias

Toward the end of summer, take a look at what your outdoor beds offer for your indoor garden. Long unrooted sprays of nasturtiums will bloom for weeks in a vase of water in a sunny window. If you have trailing lantanas, pot some of these. But my greatest garden treasure is the cascading petunias. Potted early in September, they produce fine, graceful winter bloom, the well-rooted smaller plants fitting nicely into 2½-inch pots. I take care to lift them several weeks before frost; I trim tops as much as needed for shapeliness (sometimes quite low), spray with an insecticide (just in case), and move to the shaded steps or porch for gradual acclimatizing to future indoor life. Some plants hardly miss a beat of bloom; others necessarily cut back to 2 or 3 inches wait until late February to set buds. How refreshing is the sight of these flowering summer annuals on gray winter days.

Two Vines from Seed

Then there are at least two annuals worth starting from seed for long bloom indoors. The 'Heavenly Blue' morning-glories are sown January 1. (In my experience they aren't satisfactory sown earlier and seeds don't need presoaking; they germinate better in plastic than in clay pots.) The first blue flowers open to the dot in just eight weeks and continue indefinitely. Plant ten seeds to a 4½- or 6-inch pot, then discard all but three or four of the stronger seedlings. Insert a 24-inch bamboo stake in each pot. Wind the tendrils round and round the stake and back on themselves for a nice pyramidal plant rather than a spindly wanderer, or make a teepee of growth with three stakes. Place in full sun and cut off faded blooms. (I hope you won't have white-fly trouble; both morning-glories and petunias are sometimes, not always, prone; frequent syringing at the sink and an occasional spray with malathion or one of the aerosol bombs usually keep plants clean. Anyway, don't let an attack go unchecked or you will surely lose your plants.)

Sown at the same time as the morning-glories, January 1, the black-eyed-Susan vine, *Thunbergia alata,* in mixture is not likely to bloom until late March. What a joy this is when the stake in the 4-inch pot is a mass of turning tendrils, and five-petaled, dark-centered, cream-to-orange flowers dot the foliage. Not given to trouble, this vine needs plenty of sunshine and water and brings lively canary shades to the pink, coral, and purple window picture.

12

TREATISE ON SMALL TREASURES

Minis and Dwarfs for the Fun of It

From almost every familiar species of houseplant come now miniature and semi-miniature forms that are most endearing. Why these small treasures excite so much admiration and are such a delight to grow—though most are more difficult than their full-sized parents—is hard to say. Perhaps it is that small things appeal—puppies, kittens, and ducklings; perhaps, with smaller houses, enthusiastic indoor growers find they can have variety only with a selection of definitely dwarf specimens; perhaps it is the need of apartment dwellers, now so vast in number, that has made plant breeders aware of the importance of selecting and propagating the minis and semi-minis that occur by chance or on purpose in their propagation benches. Apparently the minis are a great convenience there. Lyndon Lyon, the specialist in miniature saintpaulias, writes that "rare genetic combinations can be achieved with the miniatures in *limited* bench space and results can later be easily transferred to standard-sized plants."

The offerings of the last decade have certainly been multiple. Let's look first at the small things that bloom prolifically at windows and under lights. (Growing them in terrariums is discussed under "Random Thoughts" at the back of this book.)

African-violets

Diminutive African-violets certainly come first in popularity with

Above left, 'Baby Dear,' a 4-inch miniature African-violet; *above right, Saintpaulia magungensis minima,* the tiny species from which miniature trailers are being developed. Lyndon Lyon photos. *Center left,* a shower of pink blooms covers the brown-chartreuse leaves of the dwarf begonia 'Cleopatra' ('Maphil'); *center right,* 'Silver Jewel' is just that, a dwarf begonia with emerald-green leaves puckered silver. Walter Haring photos. *Below right,* a miniature rose in full bloom in winter is a sweet sight. Merry Gardens photo small editions of most types and colors now available. Lyndon is even perfecting some tiny trailers which particularly appeal to me as they hang down from the narrowest of my glass shelves. His miniatures—'Tiny Pink,' 'Tiny Blue,' 'Tiny Phantasy,' 'Tiny Ellie,' 'Baby Pink,' 'Baby Dear,' 'Little Cheer,' and 'Yankee Doodle'—open full-sized blooms about 1½ inches above pot rims on plants of small stature with diminutive foliage. If you are exhibiting, keep in mind that plants classed as true miniatures measure no more than 6 inches across, the semi-miniatures 8 inches.

Culture for these small versions is much the same as for the larger African-violets—temperatures of 70 to 72 degrees, plenty of natural light or winter sun, or 14 to 16 hours of artificial light, the tops of the plants about 5 inches below. If your trays are accommodating standard plants as well, set the minis on inverted pots to bring them closer to the light source. And watch out for suckers; the miniatures incline to suckering more than standard plants and for perfect form these suckers must be constantly and carefully removed.

Prepare a porous potting medium with plenty of sand or perlite mixed with your soil, which should be "sterile" (pasteurized) as for your big violets. Keep plants in as small pots as possible. In too large pots many of the little ones tend to be more than miniature. I am struggling with square plastic 1¼'s that came in a package of individual frozen fruit-juice servings; others are using thimbles! African-violets also look adorable in 1¼-inch thumb pots if you can locate these and have the patience to cope with them. Otherwise 1½- to 2-inch pots will serve.

Hold on to the thin lightweight little pots Lyndon Lyon ships his miniatures in. With tin snips, you can cut these to fit brandy snifters or those little covered glass bowls that come at Christmas with green and red berries. Cut round and round, as if you were peeling an apple, until the pot is the inch depth you want; don't cut down or you will split the pots as I did on my first try. Some collectors show off their miniatures in demitasse cups, but drilling holes in these without shattering the cups is a delicate business. Experiment with a cup from the dime store, not your best china.

Instead of shifting plants on, if growth seems to indicate, replace old soil with fresh and, if possible, return plants to the same tiny pots. Repotting three or four times a year gives best results. Gently shake off the old soil, and maybe prune roots a little with a sharp scissors to help fit your miniatures back into the same pots.

You will need to water frequently, for these small pots hold only a little soil and so dry out quickly; but don't drown your miniatures, for the absorption capacity of the roots is very limited. Some people water with an eye dropper but that's pretty tedious. Flow from my long-spouted watering can is sufficiently controlled, I find, and I fertilize as I water, of course with a very weak solution. I notice these tiny ones are very dependent on humidity. The pebble tray or glass bowl is essential, and regular fogging with an atomizer spray always gratefully received.

When it comes to starting new plants from leaf cuttings, you are really in the doll department. In spring, take leaf cuttings with ½-inch petioles (stems) and, when root systems appear large enough to manage on their own, separate the infinitesimal plantlets. These little ones grow more slowly than standard violets but still you must watch out for suckers. Patience and skillful fingers are essential in these early stages.

The semi-miniatures may suit you better. They are still relatively small plants. I prize my pretty white 'Winter Snow' and purple 'Blast Off' and they are a lot easier to handle than the tiny ones.

Other Gesneriads

Related to the saintpaulia are delectable gesneriad miniatures that rarely exceed 2 inches. Among them is the tiny species, *Sinningia pusilla,* called the miniature gloxinia. In a thimble or in a thumb pot, it is perfection, the five-petaled lavender flowers rising about an inch from a perfect rosette of olive-green foliage. Bloom is constant, the individual blossoms lasting at least a week. 'Wood Nymph' is a tiny almost white sinningia, 'Bright Eyes' an orchid shade, the plant growing somewhat taller than *S. pusilla* but still definitely miniature.

'Cupid's Doll,' 'Dollbaby,' and 'Cindy' are others in the gloxinia orbit and a lovely trio. 'Tom Thumb' is a true miniature of the florists' familiar gloxinia, red with a white-bordered corolla in nice contrast to these other pastels. For the most part, treat them all as you do African-violets. Provide even more humidity if you can; they are excellent plants for brandy glasses or open terrariums. They will thrive even at a north window, for they do not require the full light of African-violets.

Miniature and Dwarf Begonias

Enchanting are the tiny begonias, the up to 6-inch miniatures and up to 10-inch dwarfs. Even a small bright window can accommodate a number and so give you a variety of plants, even a begonia collection, in a limited space. If you can provide quite constant attention, you can grow the smallest ones in 1½-inch plastic pots, or more conveniently in 2's, but 2¼'s are usually the outside limit. With so little soil, you have to be watchful to prevent drying out and you have to fertilize regularly. If you give food at almost every watering as I do, measure it to less than the quarter strength for the larger houseplants. In general, these small begonias are not fast growers and just a little pinching and pruning will produce shapely plants.

Catalogues list a tempting selection of miniature begonias that will bloom winter and spring, among them 'Baby Perfectifolia,' 'Bow Joe,' the eyelash *B. boweri,* 'China Doll,' 'Robert Shatzer,' and *B. rotundifolia.* Rex types include 'Dew Drop,' 'Granny,' and 'Wood Nymph,' this one with tiny ivylike leaves.

Among the dwarfs that grow a little taller than the miniatures are 'Black Falcon,' 'Cathedral' (a big name for such a small plant), 'Cleopatra' ('Maphil'), 'Red Shot,' 'Silver Jewel,' 'Rosie Murphyski,' and 'It,' a silver-spotted Rex type.

Miniature wax begonias are still fairly rare, but sometimes a specialist will have a few plants in his greenhouse that are not listed in his catalogue. These small replicas are worth a search, for when the tiny plants are covered with bloom they are a sight indeed. The miniature 'Aloha' opens double salmon-orange flowers amidst green leaves; 'South Pacific' is an excellent bright red double semperflorens. If you are competent with the callas, 'Ruby Jewel' is a miniature of this type, the semi-double red flowers set off by white-and-green leaves.

All these tiny begonias thrive under fluorescent lights where, of course, more water and fertilizer are needed. The general recommendation is 8 to 10 inches below lights burning 12 to 14 hours, but I have also seen them flourishing 18 inches below when they were growing along with standard varieties. However, one shelf devoted to dwarfs and miniatures alone is certainly fun to tend.

Geraniums

For bright bloom in small quarters there are tiny slow-growing geraniums that you can keep small in 2- or 2½-inch pots for two to three years, provided you can manage the necessary nice balance of watering and feeding. These are very slow growing: 'Black Vesuvius,' 'Fairyland,' 'Imp,' 'Perky,' 'Ruffles,' and 'Small Fortune.' Then there are the adorable variegated miniatures, hardly of easy culture but a challenge for those who enjoy a challenge: 'Elf,' 'Greengold Kleiner Liebling,' 'Nugget,' 'Sprite,' 'Variegated Kleiner Liebling.' The rare silver-leaved 'Sprite' with coral blossoms is probably the easiest and best of these.

However, outside a greenhouse, miniatures in 2-inch pots or even the 2½-inch size are difficult, if not impossible, to handle. In a home on a shelf in a window with the full sun that most of them require for flowering, plants in such tiny pots need constant attention. There isn't much soil even in a 2½-inch pot and in bright weather this soon dries out and shallow roots can be damaged. Under such conditions, miniature geraniums often need water more than once a day. Unless you can always be on the alert, you may want to shift your newcomers to 3- or 3½-inch pots, as I do.

Dwarf plants likely to stay under 12 inches are less exciting. For good bloom in somewhat limited quarters these are most satisfactory. Two 30-inch glass shelves in my sunny Plant Room have held fifteen 3-inch pots of these. Once established, they give constant bloom except through possibly dull weeks in December and part of January. Of course, under fluorescent lights they never stop. And the advantage of the dwarf geraniums is that you can grow so many different kinds in a limited space.

The dwarfs and semi-dwarfs are by no means all of a size but any zonal geranium likely to stay under 12 inches is a small grower in comparison to a standard plant and may rightly be termed a dwarf. Miniatures may stay at 2 to 3 inches but culture, particularly pot size, greatly affects stature. Anyway you can be sure than 'Imp' won't grow as tall as 'Pigmy,' and both will be exceeded by 'Twinkle.'

There is also a vigorous so-called dwarf group, not of the stature of standard zonals but still inclined to outgrow even 4-inch pots rather quickly. However, these can well be your choice if notable smallness is not so important to you as continuous color and ease of culture. Among these free-blooming, larger dwarfs are: 'Dancer,' 'Dopey,' 'Emma Hossler,' 'Gypsy Gem,' 'Mischief,' 'Mr. Everaarts,' 'Pride,' 'Prince Valiant,' 'Robin Hood,' and 'Sparkle.'

You will enjoy these smaller geraniums blooming so well under fluorescent lights. (The big ones will bloom well too but they require more space and equipment than is practical in the average home.) What must be provided for any geranium is the equivalent of a sunny summer's day. Place your plants so that the tops are about 3 inches—closer if they don't burn—from the lights. Raise dwarfs and minis on inverted flower pots if the shelves are too low. Pinch tops to get bushy growth, and give more water and plant food than you give your window plants. You will find that bloom will be excellent with 14 to 18 hours of fluorescent light.

Orchids

Depending on the type of orchid flower you like, you can select miniatures of any kind, among them small Cattleyas (the corsage flower for banquet speakers), the lady-slipper Paphiopedilums (Cypripediums), or the lovely Oncidiums with butterfly sprays. Sizes of plants and flowers vary. Some like my *Haraella odorata* are not mini but minuscule. This tiny starfish thing, about the size of a half dollar, grows on a piece of cork bark in my bubble garden with a big plant label so it won't be overlooked.

Ascocentrum miniatum, a 3-inch plant, to 5 inches with flowers, blooms brilliant orange in the light garden in spring, a nice contrast to my whites and pastels there.

Brassavola nodosa, lady of the night, green-white and evening-fragrant, is a compact 8 to 10 inches; it blooms several times a year.

Dendrobium jenkinsii is really a wee one, only 2 inches high with golden flowers generally winter into spring.

Epidendrum tampense, brown-yellow with a purple spot, is 8 to 10 inches high when it blooms in spring; *E. vitellinum* offers bright red flowers on 8-inch plants in winter.

Neofinetia falcata, all white, fragrant, 6 to 8 inches, blooms in spring, sometimes again in fall.

Odontoglossum cervantesii opens scented pale pink flowers in drooping scapes from 6-inch plants in spring.

Ornithocephalus bicornis and *O. inflexus,* birds-head orchids, produce tiny green-and-white flowers for three to four months, starting early spring.

Phalaenopsis luddemanniana, waxy purple with white bands from midwinter into spring, grows 6 to 10 inches. *P. luedde-violacea* is another fragrant lavender to 6 inches in winter.

Also most appealing are the miniature Cymbidium hybrids that can be selected in white, yellow, pink, or red, for bloom at different times from winter to late spring. Flowers are numerous and long lasting. They are easy-to-grow terrestrial types.

You may find that these miniatures adjust more slowly than big ones to your home conditions. However, once established, they are dependable as well as amusing. Under "Random Thoughts" the taller orchids are discussed.

Roses

On a snowy late winter day miniature roses blooming in the window are a charming sight. They require at least five hours of sun, a not too warm room—60 degrees is better than 70 degrees, which is tolerated—good ventilation, and an evenly moist soil. These that I suggest are ever-blooming though the early winter crop may be somewhat sparse since plants are in a state of relative rest until the turn of the year. On that account wait until early January to fertilize.

Growing from 4 to 14 inches tall, the climbers to 30 inches or more, these plants are somehow amusing with their tiny hybrid tea or multiflora blooms, flowers we are used to seeing much larger. They seem to prefer clay pots and they do require the fairly high humidity of my pebble trays, also frequent syringing of tops to deter red-spider mites. Mildew may appear in a close atmosphere; for this, Lyndon Lyon, who has just perfected the vibrant 4-inch 'Red Fairy,' is experimenting with a spray of Lemon Joy detergent, ½ teaspoon to 3 to 4 cups of warm water. Fungus troubles are encouraged if faded blooms are not promptly removed and rot as they fall on the soil.

Like their outdoor counterparts, the mini roses are the better for enough pruning to keep them shapely and bushy. With tops 6 inches below fluorescent lights, most of them reach up fast. If they seem to be growing beyond miniature heights and are getting straggly, cut them back to 3 inches and they will be the stronger and bloom the better for the reduction. However, the new 'Red Fairy' has proved it will bloom continuously under lights and *remain short.*

For a full color range of miniature roses, you might like 'Baby Gold Star' and 'White Baby Star'; the pink 'Bo-Beep' (to only 8 inches even outdoors), coral 'Chipper,' the fragrant pink 'Sweet Fairy'; 'Red Fairy,' and 'Red Imp.' For a climber, there is the coral 'Hi-Ho' growing 2 to 3 feet tall, an outstanding little plant to catch the eye of every visitor.

Other Miniatures for Flowers and Foliage

Reading the catalogues of growers who are aware of the present enthusiasm for smaller plants, you will come upon many other miniatures to beguile you. You might do as I do: order say half a dozen each year, keeping the best, discarding the ailing or the non-flowering. Your main and best choice will probably be from the larger groups just considered but a few less commonly seen will add spice to your collection.

The flamingo-flower, *Anthurium scherzerianum,* has a charming small relative, so too the gardenia, *G. radicans* (just as challenging, I find, as the standard plant), the pink-white wax-plant, *Hoya bella,* and the yellow-flowering *Oxalis herrerae* and deep pink *O. rosea.*

You will want some of the smaller green things, too, especially the vines. I have so enjoyed my miniature ivies, especially those with variegated leaves, like the green-and-white 'Glacier' and yellow-splashed 'Goldheart.' Among the greens with interesting leaf forms are 'Green Feather' and 'Green Spear' with arrowhead foliage. Then there are three nice so-called ivies—the grape-ivy, *Cissus striata;* Kenilworth-ivy, *Cymbalaria muralis;* and German-ivy, *Senecio mikanoides.* The miniature fig, *Ficus pumila,* will climb or trail; and *Impatiens repens* is a flowering vine, dependable as all the impatiens tribe.

Among small upright foliage plants—you will need some of these if you are planting a terrarium—are the irislike *Acorus gramineus pusillus,* various bright-leaved, small editions of Josephs-coat, *Alternanthera versicolor,* marantas, peperomias, also that choice plant for contrast, the green-and-white *Caladium humboldtii.* The possibilities for an indoor garden filled exclusively with miniatures is both delightful and overwhelming, and the tiny things are also most attractive for the narrower shelves of a window garden that features plants of standard size.

13

BEST AMONG THE TENDER BULBS

Exciting Indoor Accents

Every year I like to grow an interesting bulb (tuber or corm) or two for colorful accent especially among the ferns and other foliage plants. In the course of time I've enjoyed a great many different ones, for I usually give them away at the end of winter to have space for something unfamiliar the next year. Amaryllis, the Amazon- or Eucharist-lily, the Jacobean- and glory-lilies, five callas (one year I grew seven different ones), have all given me a great deal of pleasure, not to mention the lovely fragrant French-Roman hyacinths and Paperwhite narcissus. A schedule for these two is given at the end of this chapter.

Amaryllis

Most recently I have been particularly pleased with a Dutch hybrid amaryllis 'Appleblossom.' I bought it in mid-November already potted (a nice expensive convenience) after making a difficult choice, for the gorgeous reds and pure whites also appealed. At first I kept it in a warm (70 to 75 degrees), rather dim spot, and watered it sparingly for about three weeks until growth was advanced to some 6 inches. Then I moved it to an east window, where it was a little cooler, increased the amount of water and also fertilized, but lightly.

The plant grew fast and before Christmas a lovely cluster of rose-

For Christmas, the amaryllis opens spectacular lilylike blooms. Geo. W. Parks Co. photo

striped pink flowers, each about 7 inches across, slowly opened on a tall stem, and a second flowering stem quickly advanced—all this before there was much leaf development. Then as the strap foliage pushed forth and the flowers faded (but not for several weeks), I cut back the long stems and gave more water and fertilizer to the decorative foliage plant. I kept it growing so on the porch through summer while it prepared more blooms for me for the next winter.

Late in August I stopped fertilizing and began watering less but did not check water entirely while the leaves were still green. When they were somewhat yellowed, and finally dried up, I cut them back to 2 to 3 inches and before frost brought the pot indoors and placed it on its side in the garage for a cool rest of six to eight weeks. Meanwhile I kept an eye on it and watered it every few weeks. After the rest, when a little growth appeared, I scooped what soil I could from the top of the pot, replaced it with a rich fresh mixture, and started my amaryllis on its way again. The second year it did not perform so early but I had flowers again late in January.

If you buy a bare, not a planted bulb, set it in a pot only 1 or 2 inches larger than the diameter of the bulb—usually a 6-, sometimes a 7-inch pot will do—and let a third of the bulb protrude above the soil. Water sparingly at first and move to a somewhat sunny window only after growth is well advanced.

The Amazon-lily can be brought into snowy, heavily textured and fragrant bloom two or three times a year by renewing and increasing the water supply after a several weeks' period of semirest. It makes a handsome and unusual accent for the window garden in full light; sun is not required. Jack Roche photo

AMAZON-LILY

This one, *Eucharis amazonica,* sometimes called eucharist-lily, is a member of the amaryllis family, and a rare beauty with exquisite fragrance. *It is not to be missed.* The umbels of exquisite white flowers suspended from the ends of 18-inch stems suggest daffodils. Even without bloom the plant is handsome with broad, glossy, evergreen leaves, each with its own petiole. The Amazon-lily is not for limited quarters, but a grand big plant. Allow four bulbs to a 10-inch pot or one bulb each to several 5-inch pots.

After the potting, provide a fairly warm location, 70 to 75 degrees, until buds appear, then about 65 degrees is better. A light but not sunny location is preferred. Water thoroughly after planting and fertilize regularly as you do your other plants, that is, until bloom is perfected. Then stop feeding until a new sequence is on the way and fresh growth indicates the need.

Every four to five weeks after each blooming, induce a rest, but not a dormancy, for the leaves are evergreen. Let the soil get fairly, but not entirely, dry during the rest and water at any sign of wilting. This handsome plant of repeated bloom is well worth your very early acquaintance.

Jacobean-lily

Sometimes also called Aztec-lily, *Sprekelia formosissima* balances scarlet, 6-inch butterfly blooms on 18-inch stems. Grown the same way as the amaryllis, this one is not so easily scheduled, but if you pot the bulb in October you will probably have flowers late February or March. This also needs a tight pot and fairly cool quarters; 65 to 70 degrees is about as much warmth as it will tolerate. Plants like this, too seldom grown, bring an exciting novelty to our indoor gardens.

Glory-lily

This lily, *Gloriosa superba* or *G. rothschildiana,* has been one of my most delightful finds. An unusual climber, it is simplicity itself when it comes to culture. Provide a 6-inch pot half full of houseplant soil. On this, lay the flat tuber and cover with more soil to within an inch of the top. I trained my plant on cord about 4 feet up the side of a window but you can make an effective specimen by inserting three, equidistant, 24-inch stakes around the edge of the pot with strings running from stake to stake. For support, pull the tendrils of the developing vine through the strings.

The gloriosa-lily likes my warm window. Potted early in February, it

The white calla-lily, potted in August, unfurls a velvety chalice. Merry Gardens photo

started to grow in two weeks, bloomed in three months, and continued through spring and summer until I induced a rest period in October. Left in the pot, fresh soil added at the top after the rest, the glory-lily, so aptly named, couldn't be easier. And it has such a different look from other plants, with those yellow-marked scarlet lilies suspended all over the green framework.

Calla-lilies

The seven of my early excitement are apparently not all available today but there are five at least from which to select. However, they are not for the very warm living room, but require cooler quarters, 55 to 60 degrees at the dim start, and less than 70 degrees once they are growing and budding. If you have a long, deep cool window, grow a pair of the big whites or yellows to show off at each end in gilded ceramic containers. They will look handsome indeed. Or plan to enliven your cool sunroom with groups of any of them.

The white *Zantedeschia aethiopica* grows about 3 feet tall and produces arrow-shaped leaves as striking as the flowers. For Christmas bloom, pot bulbs in August. You can count on four or five flowers from each tuber and the effect will be fresh and charming for almost two weeks.

Growing only to 2 feet, *Z. albo-maculata,* called the spotted calla for the white markings on the green leaves, is also potted in August and both are brought to dormancy by reducing water toward the end of June.

The golden calla, *Z. elliottiana,* is another giant with glorious 5-inch flowers, but usually only one to a tuber, and silver-spotted leaves. Wait until November to pot this one. Grow it cool, even below 60 degrees, and expect bloom near Easter time. It requires about four months after potting to produce its golden perfection and a rest period from early June on.

The pink-to-red calla, *Z. rehmannii,* is a charming 12-inch species and so fits in better with your other houseplants if these are in a fairly cool location. It produces a fine winter display over a three-week period. The tubers may be potted at almost any time but October always seems best to me for handling the indoor bulbs.

For a rare accent, there is *Z. melanoleuca* (*Z. tropecalis*), the "black"-throated yellow calla. You plant the stony bit hoping you have it right side up but, if not, when growth starts you can carefully reverse it. Green points show in about three weeks and grow until the plant reaches about 20 inches.

Provide 6-inch pots for the two tall callas, 4-inch for the other three. Set the bulbs deep in pots of fairly heavy loam mixed with a third of leafmold or humus. Allow ample space at the top of the pots to receive water, for once callas gain their growth they require quantities, usually twice-a-day applications. I set my plants in soup bowls and fill these with water that the thirsty plants soon drain away.

Moisten new calla plantings and set them in a cool place where light is dim. They will need little water until top growth appears in three to four weeks. Then move the pots to light and warmth (but under 70 degrees) and fertilize as you do your other plants. When the flower stalk emerges, give the plants full sun but move them out of the sun as flowers are perfected. Full sun at the bloom stage hastens fading.

After the summer's rest, lift and clean the tubers and repot in October or November, according to the nature of each, and start the beautiful cycle all over again. Calla tubers have a practically indefinite life so your investment pays dividends for as long as your own interest lasts.

French-Roman Hyacinths and Paperwhite Narcissus

French-Roman hyacinths are choice. Dainty, with smaller, more widely spaced bells than the stalwart Dutch type, they have the same delicious scent and are selected by color—pink, blue, or white. In the course of three weeks in my living room, each rooted bulb produces as many as six lovely sprays. (If your living room is pretty warm, move the bowls to cooler night quarters to prolong the freshness of the flowers.)

I arrange the bulbs in matching bowls of pebbles and water (peatmoss is as good), and set them at the start in the cold, *not freezing,* garage or pantry. There the water level is frequently checked to be sure it reaches the base of the bulbs but not much above. First plantings take about ten weeks. Such a joy the hyacinths are at Thanksgiving and Christmas. I keep them in the garage for the first five or six weeks and find that the later the planting, the less time it takes for bloom. Bulbs may mold if kept from rooting, so plant no later than mid-November. (However, if you want to hold some for late January fragrance, store the bulbs cold, just above freezing.) I have also grown the so-called fairy hyacinths, 'Borah' and 'Blue Star,' but they have only a light fragrance, and the pink 'Rosalie' apparently has none. Also, while they bloom well, they tend to bunchy stalks, lacking the open grace of the French-Roman hyacinths. I really do not like them.

Narcissus grandiflora, the familiar Paperwhites, are scheduled according to my pleasure. They look lovely on the broad living-room window and offer sweet fragrance among scentless poinsettias, cyclamens, and green plants. Just one opening cluster scents a room. Blooms last for weeks if the bowls are moved to a cooler place at night.

I get in my supply of *N. grandiflora* in September. The Paperwhites started mid-month begin to open by Thanksgiving, requiring ten weeks in all then but proportionately less time as the season advances. (Put bulbs in the refrigerator, *not the freezer,* or in a cold pantry that is about 40 degrees, if you want to hold them for first-of-February bloom; so late in the season, they take only four weeks overall and look very pretty on short stems.)

Lately, I have had trouble getting satisfactory stock. Apparently the only reliable bulbs are imported from southern France, so try to get a supplier who can furnish the French-grown bulbs in *large* sizes, and do order early. In any case, don't buy bulbs late in the season from an open basket in a florist shop, department store, or supermarket. They will be dried out and most unlikely to bloom.

My friend Lois Wilson, who has had spectacular success with Paperwhites, soaks the bulbs for half an hour in a Rapid-Gro starter solution before planting them *directly* in a deep pebble garden in the living room. As they come into bloom, she gives them a full-strength dose of Rapid-Gro. She reports that in some years there has been little scent on the early plantings but a marvelous pervading fragrance from the later ones.

I have not had such good results with direct plantings. I get better blooms and shorter foliage if the planted bulbs spend the first two weeks in a dark, cool place and are then gradually brought to light and sun. Pebbles are still my favorite medium, either the white ones, called roofing pebbles, or pea gravel from a building-supply company. Of course, the large, polished river-washed ovals are prettiest of all.

I have grown the white-and-yellow Chinese sacred-lily and the golden 'Soleil d'Or' narcissus, sometimes called yellow Paperwhites. These are somewhat slower, for February and March, when they are charming in a deep window with great jars of forced forsythia set among them.

Discard these tender bulbs once they have bloomed. They can only survive and bloom again in gardens in the South.

A Winter Schedule

For Thanksgiving	French-Roman Hyacinths (start September 5 to 10) Paperwhite Narcissus (start mid-September)
For Christmas	French-Roman Hyacinths (start mid-October) Paperwhite Narcissus (start mid-November)
For January	French-Roman Hyacinths (start November 1 but keep cold till January 1) Paperwhite Narcissus (start 3 to 4 weeks ahead)

14

FLORIST PLANTS WITH FINE FUTURES

Long Life for Gift Plants

Handsome flowering and fruiting plants from the florist bring welcome winter color to living room and window garden. Some have a very long present and a permanent future if you wish to take the trouble to carry them through summer. All of them will give you weeks, some months, of bloom if properly cared for. The week after Christmas I grieve to see poinsettias losing their leaves; the denuded plants that a few days ago brought such bright seasonal greetings now suggest the most gloomy prospects for the coming year. Or perhaps it is a limp cyclamen that depresses me, for there are probably some fifty buds that might have opened in the right location. Such disasters can so easily be avoided. Here is some specific advice on your gift plants. However, since their basic requirements are like those of most other houseplants, won't you glance again at the Seven Keys to Success discussed in Chapter 5.

POINSETTIA. The seven- to ten-day beauty of the old red type has been extended to five months or more by new Mikkelsen and Eckes varieties in pink and white as well as red. You may still prefer red, but if plants are going to hold blooms, you may get tired of the Christmas red-and-green effect all through spring. My large and small plants of 'Mikkelpink' hold their colorful bracts (the flowers are those inconspicuous yellow clusters in the center) until late May. Red varieties will do as well. The lovely greenish-white ones so far have not held beyond two months. These I discard when they fade as not being promising enough to hold over.

I enjoy poinsettias with other Christmas plants at cool living-room windows (thermostat at 65 degrees at night) through the holidays. Then I move them to the Plant Room where nights are well below 65 degrees. If a little shoot starts just below the bloom, I cut it off. Brackets will promptly fade if these shoots are allowed to grow.

My poinsettias go outside in June; if yours lose their bracts much sooner and you want to hold plants for next year, set them in the till-after-frost interim in a 50- to 60-degree place and water just enough to avoid bone-dryness. Outdoors remove any ferns that may have come with a big plant and pot them separately, for these ferns, usually *Pteris tremula,* can be useful. Cut back poinsettia tops to about 3 inches. When I get to it—there's no great rush about this—I repot in a fresh soil mixture, returning plants if possible to the same pots. Big plants can be divided, and I do prefer single specimens and select them at Thanksgiving if I am buying my own. Singles are easier to associate with other plants or to place, as I sometimes do, a pair of pink ones on each side of a big rose-colored cyclamen.

Through summer, as the poinsettias thrive in a light open place near the porch, they are regularly watered and fed weekly with a liquid fertilizer. As new leaves form, stems are pinched back frequently to keep growth low. Early in September plants are moved to the porch, then brought inside about mid-month. Since poinsettias are short-day, long-night plants, to bloom they must have at least twelve hours of *certain* darkness for some seventy days—not even a gleam from a street light. I move mine to a guest-room closet every night—8 P.M. to 8 A.M. is the dark schedule—then back to the cool, sunny Plant Room for the day. With the same schedule your gift plant of one year can become your permanent houseplant for years to come, and the satisfaction of reblooming this gift plant is considerable.

CYCLAMEN. Grow this one cold, not merely cool. I've yet to see a cyclamen in a warm living room that wasn't fainting. People blame the florist. The truth is the cyclamen can't stand heat. Grown at 45 degrees (night) and 60 to 65 degrees in full light *with soil kept quite wet,* it will open every tiny bud for five months or more. Sometimes when I set plants out in June, they go on blooming for weeks. What a plant! But by July they must be induced to rest. Gradually withhold water and put the plant—the pot turned on its side—outdoors in the shade of a shrub.

The cyclamen will give a repeat performance every winter for years if you want it to, and if you are given something lovely like a fringed rose-feathered white, you will want to hold on to it. This is the way to do it. Let it rest, almost, not quite, dry until August when new sprouts

Left, in fruit in fall, in fragrant flower in spring, a dwarf orange is delightful for a cool but heated sunroom where there is space for it. Merry Gardens photo. *Right,* this little tree, *Ardisia crispa,* holds scarlet fruits in one layer with new growth at the top and white blooms below in June. Alfred Byrd Graf photo

appear. Then clean off the top growth and rest the corm, with some old soil clinging to it, so that it protrudes about ½ inch above the soil surface, almost in line with the pot rim. You can probably use the same pot, filling in with a fresh soil mixture.

Well before frost, bring your cyclamen in to a cool east window or set it to the fore of your plant tray in a south window where other plants next the glass get the sunlight. Keep your plant well nourished. As it grows, I follow my usual procedure of watering each time with a weak solution of fertilizer.

I admit that I get pretty good results with less than ideal temperatures for both poinsettias and cyclamens. They appear happy together in the Plant Room—a matter of compromise, I suppose—the poinsettia a little cooler than it prefers, the cyclamen a little warmer.

KALANCHOE. Like most succulents, this one, *K. blossfeldiana,* wants but little here below except twelve to fourteen hours of darkness every night for three weeks before Christmas—if you want it to bloom then. Like the poinsettia, it is a short-day plant. So I hustle mine off to the dark closet around Thanksgiving, then to a sunny window about December 15. Here it blooms repeatedly, holding good color for weeks. If the first crop of faded flowers is cut off low down, more soon push up, and this goes on until May. The kalanchoe doesn't mind living-room heat at 72 degrees or a little more if nights are cooler. Nor does it require high humidity or even pebble-tray treatment. I provide a gritty soil, about half humus and half perlite, and very little fertilizer; I water it less than other plants, letting soil dry out usually for three days between waterings. The kalanchoe must be assured fresh air; in a hot, close atmosphere mealy bugs cluster under the thick overlapping leaves and close to the stems. Get rid of them at the start with an alcohol-dipped swab since kalanchoes won't tolerate a big clean-up with malathion. A semishaded place in summer is good.

Some year you might like to feature these plants in your window garden. A number of hybrids as well as more species have recently become available. There is the dwarf 'Yellow Tom Thumb,' the full-sized 'Jingle Bells' in coral tones, and *K. fedtschenkoi marginata* 'Tricolor,' a trailer with blue-gray, white, and pink foliage and pink flowers. The kalanchoes are well worth rediscovering.

CHRISTMAS-CACTUS, *Schlumbergera bridgesii*. Not from the desert but from the mountains of Brazil, this handsome Christmas plant can be a treasure for years. Your florist plant will probably be in a 5-inch pot and lovely with perhaps a dozen pendant fuchsialike blooms in rich red-purple tones. I set mine on a bracket in a sunny window so that the fountainous growth shows to advantage for the four to six weeks when every leaf tip is lit with bloom.

To give you pleasure in subsequent years, a certain regime must be followed. When there are no more buds to open, grow the plant somewhat dry, and prune off a link or two from each branch to promote shapeliness. In summer provide a somewhat shaded spot in the garden or on the porch. *Insist on a complete rest in October*. Set the plant in a dim cold place and withhold water for the whole month. In November water twice, once early in the month, once mid-month. At the end of November I move my Christmas-cactus in with the other window-garden plants, at first a little back from the sun, then where it can benefit from the full beams. At first, water is applied weekly, then about every other day with the same fertilizer solution as for the other plants, sometimes less often, depending on the weather. As buds form, watering is always checked a little because a too wet soil loosens them.

So treated, your plant at the window may not bloom until January. Like the poinsettia, it wants a long night. For earlier flowers, I put this one also in the dark closet for twelve to thirteen hours every night from the first of December till buds show color.

THANKSGIVING OR CRAB-CACTUS, *Zygocactus truncatus*. This is the one with teeth or claws at the ends of the "chain" growth. There's a lot

At Christmas the cool, sunny window ledge of the living room holds a lively (and lasting) collection of favorite gift plants—white cyclamens, a pink poinsettia, bowls of Paperwhite narcissus (these started mid-November); *at the far left,* a small-leaved ivy on a double wire arch; *at the far right,* an indispensable angel-wing begonia in bloom; *on the latch strip* a trailing begonia, and elsewhere wax begonias, a spider-plant, and ferns of different forms and textures. George C. Bradbury photo

of difference in the plants acquired under this name. If you can get a slip from a plant that blooms when you would like it to, that's a good idea. Mine flowers on the button at Thanksgiving and often again in spring, the color orangey red. I grow it cold and dry in the fall like the Christmas-cactus but it comes into the house sooner as I see buds forming in the November cold on the porch.

AZALEA. This is a valuable shrub, expensive like the cyclamen and worth holding on to, I think. Usually I receive this at Easter, not Christmas, and the pink, white, or blush blooms appear again at about the same time the next year. The azalea needs to be grown cool, below 60 degrees if possible. To get the great crop of buds to open and not lose a single one, take care soil doesn't dry out, for the roots are manifold and demanding. You may need to water more than once a day and certainly once a week also submerge the pot until the topsoil feels moist. I fertilize this one with Miracid.

For the in-bud florist azalea, an east or west window is a perfect location with sun in moderation. There you should get two months or more of bloom depending on how heavily your plant is budded. Nip off the faded flowers.

Set your plant outdoors for the summer. I repot mine in rich acid compost as soon as it goes out and usually, not always, I can get it back into the same pot. Too many big plants just can't be accommodated and azaleas are usually already in the shallow 6- or 7-inch so-called azalea pots. Outdoors in partial shade in the myrtle bed beside the porch, the azalea is not out of sight, out of mind but in plain view and assured of a good soaking if any week is without rain. Late in June it is pruned to shapeliness, the tips of the branches cut back.

The azalea also spends October on the cool shaded porch. Since fall is a somewhat dormant period, it is watered less then, though never allowed to dry out. About mid-November, I bring it indoors to a cold sunny window where it stays until flower buds begin to appear in January or February. Then it is moved next the glass of the south window of the Plant Room and fertilized with Miracid solution as new growth develops. The top is syringed at the sink when the plant gets the required deep weekly soaking. Such top syringing is essential to prevent an attack of red-spider. Lovely through months of bloom in its second year, the gift azalea is well worth the effort of this holdover.

GLOXINIA. This handsome relative of the African-violet will bloom for three to four months, a brilliant accent plant in living room or window garden. It thrives under the same conditions as the saintpaulia and also likes the winter sunlight but a shaded location in summer. Once it has opened all its buds, it may develop a second cycle of bloom if you cut off the stem above the lowest two good leaves and water it only lightly for about a month. If no new growth develops, stop watering altogether until tops wither. Then store the pot in a cool place, under 60 degrees, and water just enough, about once a month, to avoid complete dryness. The gloxinia, unlike the evergreen African-violet, is now in a dormant condition that will last for weeks or even months. Don't forget it but don't overwater either or that buried dormant tuber will rot.

When sprouts appear, a new cycle of growth is indicated. Repot the tuber in fresh soil, in the same squatty 5-inch pot if possible, otherwise in just one size larger. Bring it indoors well before frost to a sunny window and rotate it there so it will grow evenly. If it gets leggy through the dull early winter days, cut it back to the lowest pair of leaves early in March and it will grow bushy again in the stronger spring sunlight. Water and feed it as you do your African-violets and you will have a flowering plant of many years' beauty.

CHRYSANTHEMUMS. These gift plants are now brought into bloom every month in the year. I'd prefer to receive mine in the fall, which is the natural season when chrysanthemums look right. Blooming in spring, they always appear somewhat bewildered. Whenever you receive them, they will be attractive for three weeks or longer, depending on the number of buds and the coolness of the location; 60 degrees is best. Water deeply, submerging the pot as for azaleas, and spray tops to discourage aphids. Watch out for these. I once received a handsome gift plant that developed aphids before I even noticed the attack. Of course, nearby plants were well infested. Did I get busy!

If you have garden space and want to hold over your chrysanthemums, cut tops back to a couple of inches after flowering and move the plant to a cold cellar or above-freeezing garage. There water it just enough to keep soil from drying out completely; set the plant out in a garden bed late in spring. It may or may not pull through winter; some florist chrysanthemums are hardy, some are not.

Perhaps you will receive a cineraria or calceolaria. If there are many buds, put your plant in the sun; if plants are at their height of bloom—as they are likely to be—a light *cool* place is best to prevent fast fading. When flowering is over, discard the plants.

RED-FRUIT PLANTS. The shrubby Christmas-pepper, *Capsicum baccatum,* and Christmas- or Jerusalem-cherry, *Solanum pseudo-capsicum,* will hold fruits only in a cold place, 50 to 60 degrees. In a warm place, you soon hear a cannonade of falling peppers and cherries. In a cool vestibule, either will be a welcome sight through early winter. When good looks pass, discard; neither costs very much, and holding them over really isn't worth while.

But cherish the coral ardisia, *Ardisia crispa.* This little tree revels in full sun and by June is delightful. The scarlet fruits still hold in bunches among shining leaves with a cloud of white bloom just above, and new growth pushing forth at the very top adding up to a three-layer effect. Grown cool, assured deep watering, the usual liquid fertilizer, and a summer outdoors, this small evergreen can be a permanent houseplant for you, and it is handsome indeed.

CITRUS FRUITS. Orange and lemon trees add the charm of fragrant flowers to the interest of colorful fruit. Grow these in the spring sunshine but no warmer than 65 degrees, and 50 degrees is better, until fall when you see the fruits are coloring. From fall through January, plants rest but hold their fruits. Then comes a big spurt of scented bloom in March. Prune to keep shapely. Move outdoors after frost and repot, replacing topsoil then with a rich, fresh mixture. Always water deeply as you do all shrubby plants by the pot-submergence method.

15

THEIR GOING OUT AND THEIR COMING IN

Holidays for Houseplants

Outdoor summers for houseplants are a fine thing like camp for children and sea breezes for adults. Health and beauty are promoted if proper locations are found and the potted plants regularly tended and not forgotten. Protection from wind is essential, as is protection from flooding, if that is possible. Heavy rains such as we had in the hurricane days of 1972 almost ruined some of my pot plants, although they were placed in the myrtle bed on inverted saucers to avoid too much moisture from below, as well as the depredations of tunneling worms that upset drainage arrangements. Day after day the plants were drenched, and it was not possible to bring them into the porch, which was already well tenanted, perhaps too heavily so. Eventually I set them on the steps where they dried out in the sun.

Their Going Out

Before choosing locations, certain decisions are made and certain plants that have been less than happy or new ones I find I don't care for very much are discarded or bestowed. Those to be held over are given a good pest-control spraying although trouble indoors may disappear under ideal outdoor conditions. However, some nearby garden plants may not be entirely pest-free so the precaution is wise. And I hope you never let

Outdoors in summer, the fancy-leaved geraniums revel in an open area with some sun to which they are gradually exposed. Here a broad stump serves as base for a great tub of two fancy-leaved geraniums, 'Mrs. Henry Cox' and 'Prince Bismarck,' with *Pelargonium graveolens* 'Dark Red Irene,' and the sprawling *P. reniforme*. In the ground tub are *P. crispum* 'Prince Rupert,' 'Silver Lining,' *P. graveolens* 'Rober's Lemon Rose,' and the ivy-leaved geranium 'Mexican Beauty,' all still in pots but packed in peatmoss. Those that grow too big for indoor accommodations will be passed on to friends with larger plant rooms. George C. Bradbury photo

On the porch buffet table, outside the living-room window, a big Mexican basket sets off the large grape-ivy; and a pair of inquiring ceramic pigeons make the picture. Charles Marden Fitch photo

A lightly shaded bed of myrtle offers healthful holiday quarters, the foliage of the groundcover preventing mud splashing, as in an open bed. Here, the holly and other ferns, spider-plants, the upright Swedish-ivy, and a kohleria enjoy outdoor air and humidity. George Taloumis photo

gladiolus come near your houseplants, for these are thrip-prone. Heliotrope and lantana must be checked for white fly, but I want both plants for the window garden.

Outside positions in sun are chosen according to the natural preference of the plants—the geraniums to open locations in full sun on the front-

A basket of luxuriant rabbits-foot fern hangs from the arbor beams, benefiting from early eastern sunshine and the afternoon shade of the wisteria vine. Watering is by ladder, of course. George Taloumis photo

Outside the guest-room window a basket of fuchsias summers in the open shade. Against the house, under a plaque of classic figures that I like to associate with my plants, is a wall vase of blue-flowered *Lobelia* 'Blue Cascade.' George Taloumis photo

door platform, along the south edge of the Look-Into Garden, or in the open on tree stumps beside the brook. Wherever the sun-lovers go, they must be acclimated gradually or they will faint with the brightness, droop despite watering, and lose some leaves.

Unless you plan to bring them in again—and you may not want tremendous specimens back in the house—remove the pots and let them have a summer's fling with ranging roots until frost spells finis. Of course, if these are favorites, you will want to take cuttings either when you put them out or late in August. Geraniums like 'Patricia Andrea' and 'Shocking' and 'Toyon' are always outgrowing me, so I employ them as handsome bedding plants in the summer sun.

In Light Shade

Begonias, impatiens, and the foliage plants are placed in light shade. I like a bed well furnished with groundcover for the potted plants. Then mud does not splash them. And how the wax begonias and the impatiens thrive. Neither rain nor summer heat phases them, fresh and perky, the

The flagstone platform and the myrtle bed shaded by the fringe-tree offer other summer quarters for houseplants. Geraniums in pots, in a planter, and in a hanging basket revel in the summer sun. The stand holds small foliage plants, including false-aralia; a cut-leaf philodendron is silhouetted against the white house; other plants parade down the steps toward the shade. George C. Bradbury photo

whites whiter than ever, the pinks deepening their tones as they go on blooming and blooming, producing even more heavily than in winter when they certainly also did very well. Of course, they are cut back to 2 to 3 inches but they soon renew their tops. And I speed them on—and all the plants going outdoors for that matter—with a good dose of liquid plant food right at the start.

If the houseplants are placed near the porch or front steps and preferably near a hose, you won't neglect them, even if the heat makes every effort monumental. I keep a nozzle on a hose at the front-door rack and spray the plants in the sun there *early* every morning unless there has been adequate rainfall. The plants in the shade near the house may need me only every other day. Those in the myrtle bed beside the porch are also on a every-other-day schedule. In the light open shade of the May-tree, the English hawthorn, they don't dry out so fast.

The big basket plants hanging from the arbor—ferns, vines, and fuchsias—require a tremendous amount of water. Since this must be administered by ladder, I try to figure their needs and schedule my

In summer, at the south end on the screened porch, a decorative grouping of houseplants thrives with glimpses of sunshine. The hanging ceramic holds *Aeschynanthus* 'Black Pagoda'; the basket, lamium. On the iron pedestal is my indestructible rabbits-foot fern. The white stand from the Plant Room supports a miscellany, taking their ease and storing vitality for next winter indoors. George Taloumis photo

In a more protected corner of the porch are grouped the tall, well-staked *Begonia* 'Corallina de Lucerna' (having outgrown me, it will go to a friend in September), my big needle asparagus-fern, and a spider-plant. The hanging ceramic holds *Columnea* 'Sylvia.' Outside, against the house, a plaque of the Virgin and Child completes the picture. George Taloumis photo exertions accordingly. I soak tops and soil until water drips through the bottom. In very dry, sunny, breezy weather when evaporation is rapid, this can be a twice-a-day business, otherwise every other day suffices.

On the Porch

An open veranda or screened porch is a healthful location for plants in summer and a place where you can thoroughly enjoy them. Suspended in the corners, from beams at each end of the meeting-house bench, or set on the buffet shelf outside the living-room window, they make a verdant bower of the enclosed room. Upright plants adorn the wire stand outdoors in summer as they do indoors in winter. The glass table in the center holds the terrarium of small treasures, and little begonia specimens and vases of rooting cuttings go nicely on end tables.

Sometimes I bring the African-violets out for a month or so but they don't care for high heat and humidity and are subject to a mite infestation as I discovered to my sorrow one blazing summer, so I mostly keep them inside where it is cooler. In summer, as in winter, potted plants are decorative whether they accent garden beds or transform the porch where every leisure hour is the more delightful for their presence.

Their Coming In—Pot Plants and Garden Plants

Depending on your climate, the pot plants usually have to be collected and conditioned for indoor life early in September. Cold nights retard growth and a touch of frost can finish them. It's a good idea to assemble them early on the steps or the porch, for gradual acclimating to indoor conditions. If you bring plants too quickly from full sun and humidity to diffused light and a dryer atmosphere, they will inevitably develop yellow leaves or lose them altogether.

For these reasons, don't delay much after Labor Day. Scrub the pots, go over the tops for any dead leaves, prune a little perhaps for shapeliness, and give a thorough insecticide spraying, reaching the underside as well as the tops of the leaves. I hope you attended to most of the necessary repotting before the summer holiday. Plants recover so much more quickly when they are going out to ideal conditions than when they are coming in to home life.

The first weeks indoors, keep windows and doors open as weather permits, be sure the plant trays are filled with water, and fog foliage frequently to compensate for the less humid atmosphere indoors. With such care your potted houseplants will be off to a fine start and probably not miss a beat.

I have also found it possible to lift certain plants from the garden and pot them for continuous bloom indoors. Both wax begonias and impatiens, big plants and volunteer seedlings, are potted early in September and grouped on the front steps in the light shade of the fringe-tree. I keep a watering can beside them and *three or four times a day I sprinkle the tops.* Even if they wilt from the transplanting, they perk up and go on opening buds. I keep them on the steps for ten days or so until nights begin to get quite cold. Then I bring them to the Plant Room, set them on the pebble trays, and fog the tops frequently. The front door stays open through the day and the windows are partly open at night to minimize the change of climate. With this procedure, I have the benefit of the same plants for several years, in the garden in summer, in the house in winter. This treatment won't work with all plants, certainly not with geraniums, but it is worth a try.

16

MORE OF THE SAME
Easy Methods of Propagation

On shelves and tables here, there are always a few small glass vases and pitchers of rooting houseplants. Cuttings or, as we used to call them, slips, of begonias, coleus, geraniums, tradescantia, Swedish-ivy, furry lengths of the rabbits-foot fern with lacy fronds attached, and others make pretty bouquets, and the cuttings, so easily rooted in water, are always available to increase my own stock of plants—were that desirable—or to give to friends who admire some mature plant. The variegated Swedish-ivy, the green-and-white inch-plant, and 'Firebird' coleus are always in demand, as wax begonias and impatiens plants because these actually set buds even in their infancy in vases, so I am hard put to keep a supply. The dangling offsets of spider- and twelve-apostles-plants are similarly started but with a weight of pebbles to hold them down in a low bowl of water rather than in a vase.

Cuttings

Succulent growers root very quickly, so too geraniums. You can insert pieces of firm green growth in soil at the edges of a big plant and in a month you will have plants to transfer to separate pots. Another way I start them, as I have said, is in 3-inch pots of houseplant soil, the ends inserted in little clumps of sand in the center of the pots. The cuttings

Above, new plants develop when short stems of large begonia leaves are inserted in a box of sandy soil. *Below,* clusters of new plants, here ready for separation, develop at the base of each leaf cutting inserted in a pot of light soil. Jack Roche photos

The pot-in-pan device, here used for gloxinia leaves, offers an easy method for rooting cuttings under evenly moist conditions. Jack Roche photo

root in the sand in three to four weeks, then roots push out for nourishment into the soil beyond. This method, for other plants too, avoids transplanting through several pot sizes.

A plastic shoe- or breadbox, a glass casserole, just so there is a cover, a fish aquarium, or one of the popular new bubble bowls can serve as a miniature greenhouse for cuttings—for seeds also, but I think growing houseplants from seed is too much trouble. Anyway, depending on the depth of the receptacle, spread about 2 inches of small stones or coarse gravel over the bottom for drainage, then 2 inches of half-and-half sand and peatmoss, or perlite, or coarse vermiculite, whatever is handiest. Moisten this, but not to the point of sogginess, insert the cuttings, and cover, using a pane of glass for an aquarium, and set in a warm, light but not sunny place. If moisture collects, lift the cover, wipe it, and let it stay off for, say, half an hour. Then replace. After the first watering, you probably won't need to moisten the plantings ever. When roots form, lift the little plants and pot them separately in your houseplant soil.

You can be quite casual about breaking off branches for rooting or take cuttings the proper way for serious propagation. Along stems you will see tiny lumps or nodes. Cut sharply just below one of these points of growth, allowing at least two nodes and three internodes—the spaces between—to each 3- to 4-inch cutting. Select firm "middle-aged" growth, neither tough and old, nor sappy and young. With geraniums a stem makes a good cutting if, when bent, it snaps but does not quite break through, a few fibers holding. Try to avoid bruising or crushing.

Remove the lower leaves so none will touch the soil, and any little "wings" you see along the stems. Trim off flower buds and very large leaves. Without roots, cuttings can't support much top growth and are likely to wilt and perhaps rot if the leaf burden is too great. But don't take off all the leaves, for food is manufactured in them. You can dip cuttings in a rooting hormone powder if you wish before inserting them about two nodes deep in soil.

How long before rooting? It depends on the species. Often two to three weeks is long enough for roots to form for separate potting. You can "spoon" up one cutting to check and replace it unharmed if you were too optimistic. African-violet leaf cuttings make little clusters quite soon in water or soil and, when separately potted, come to blooming size, sometimes in as little as six months.

Pot-in-pan Method

Foolproof and so easy for almost all plants is the pot-in-pan device for rooting stem or mallet cuttings (a piece of stem with a single leaf as for English ivy), and for big leaves like those of begonias. In the center of an 8-inch bulb pan—the drainage hole plugged—place a corked 3-inch flower pot filled with water. Firmly pack the space between pot and pan with sand, perlite, or vermiculite. Insert cuttings of one kind or various kinds—begonias, geraniums, ivy, philodendron, poinsettia—

spaced so they do not touch. Seepage of water through the walls of the inside clay pot keeps the growing medium evenly moist; just add more water to the smaller pot as the supply diminishes. Set your pot-in-pan in a light place indoors, or on the porch, or under an arbor, but, if it's outdoors, take care to check the water supply frequently, for evaporation will be faster than in the house.

New Plants from Leaves

African-violets are the classic example of propagation by means of leaves. To root one violet leaf, use a 2¼-inch pot filled with pasteurized potting soil (or other rooting medium such as vermiculite alone or mixed in equal parts with peatmoss). Prop the leaf in place with a plant label.

Cover with a drinking glass or fruit jar. Or make a miniature greenhouse from a plastic shoe- or breadbox. Insert leaves in the same growing medium as for the 2¼-inch pot and put on the cover. Roots are bound to form in the uniform humidity of the box. If moisture collects, remove the cover and wipe it dry. Then replace.

To root leaves in water, crimp foil over the top of a small glass or bottle and insert leaf stems through holes punched in the foil. When leaves have formed a good system of roots, transplant with care to a small pot of soil and provide high humidity with a drinking glass or plastic cone supported on short lead pencils. When new leaves are a third as big as the parent leaf, the young plants may be divided. Plants at the 4½- to 5-month stage are ready to be planted separately to 2¼-inch pots. Separate tender plants and roots carefully. Blooms come in six to twelve months from the time the leaf is put down to root.

The large leaf of a begonia, a Rex perhaps, will also produce progeny not only from a petiole or leaf stem, as with the African-violet, but from the actual surface of the leaf. This is the way you manage it. Cut off a mature leaf with an inch or so of stem. Then with a sharp knife notch the underside of the leaf across the main and side veins but don't tear the leaf apart. Lay it on the growing medium of pot-in-pan, or on a pot or flat of prepared soil, the stem inserted, the leaf securely held in contact by a few pebbles or broken bits of flower pot on top. Or you can snip a very large leaf into triangles and insert the pointed ends in the sand. Either way, roots will form and a whole cluster of new leaves will appear at the slit veins or points of the triangle. As the new leaves grow and

The strawberry-geranium or -begonia, *Saxifraga sarmentosa,* sends up clouds of white blossoms from a crown of silver-veined, pink, scalloped leaves while dangling down thin stems of plantlets to root on little strategically placed pots of soil. Merry Gardens photo

the old one deteriorates, cut away the clusters and pot them. Let them gain some size before you divide them into separate plants for individual pots.

By Division

It is also possible to divide big plants, pulling the crowns apart. Or simply remove offsets or stolons as you so easily can from spider-plants or neomaricas and a few others that produce suckers. If you let African-violets develop multiple crowns, these can be divided. However, looking over my houseplants, I see very few that can be separated, some ferns perhaps, stem or leaf cuttings or offsets being the more desirable method of increase for most plants.

17

PLEASURES OF A PLANT ROOM
Mine and Others'

One mild winter morning when I was taking a meditative breather on the bench in the Round Garden, I happened to glance back at the south front of Stony Brook Cottage, flat, with the traditional New England stoop in the center, windows on each side. And a dandy idea occurred to me: Why not knock out the front door, move the steps from center to side, and build an offset to serve as a Plant Room? This could have three exposures if I installed a glass storm door on the east. Immediately I realized what an expensive flight of fancy this was and tried to clear my mind of it. In the twenty years I had lived here I had already changed the windows, raised the roof, divided the garage to make a new kitchen, and "finally" built the dining room. The thought of more building thoroughly annoyed me with myself, for I had vowed that when the new dining room was finished I'd leave this house alone.

But the vision of a Plant Room became a fixation. By August it was a reality, and what a pleasure it has been. I have always enjoyed living with plants rather than growing them in separate quarters. Now I have a sunny, three-exposure room for them—and me, a place to read the paper, hover over a Sunday breakfast tray, or write at a card table as relief from my desk. The only problem there is concentrating on anything but the plants. I rearrange, clip off leaves and blooms, water, fertilize, and climb the little ladder to check the high-up shelf plants lighted by fluorescents.

This is the comfortable sitting room that healthfully accommodates a large collection of plants on pebble trays, a plant stand, and a high-up shelf under fluorescent lights. Cream-colored paneling frames the big window. Wallpaper with a yellow pattern, a yellow rug, and yellow upholstery make a cheerful setting for plants and people. George Taloumis photo

Stony Brook Cottage before the front door was moved to the side to make way for the Plant Room. Ben Luden photo

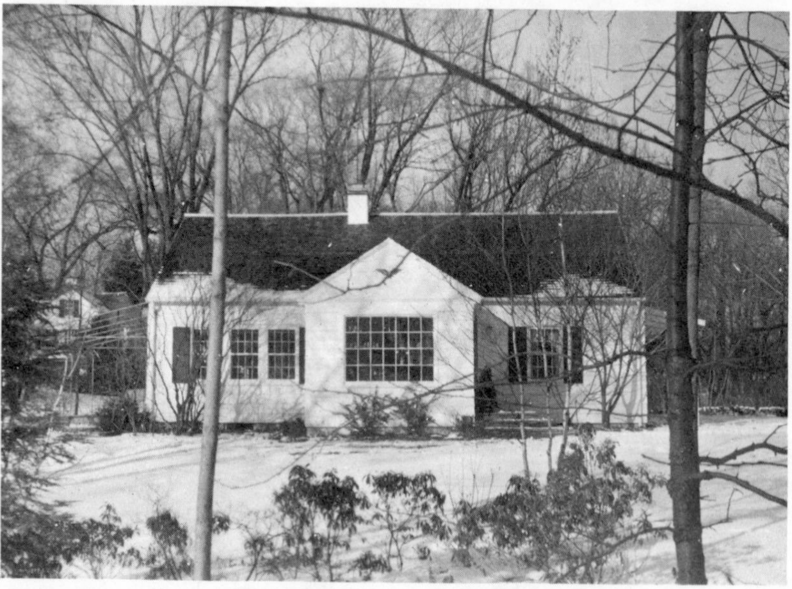

The 9- by 11-foot extension faces south with casements on the west, the big window on the south, and the front door and steps on the east. Ben Luden photo

The south window, here filled mainly with geraniums, in other years has held a collection of African-violets, or a miscellany of unfamiliar plants on trial. *At the far left,* a climbing geranium is supported on a double wire arch. George C. Bradbury photo

Construction

As you see from the before and after pictures I had the help of an experienced designer-contractor, Philip Punzelt, who knew how to keep the new room in scale with the house. The Plant Room measures 9 by 11 feet, and readily accommodates more than 100 plants as well as chairs and a table for human comfort. The long sunny 5- by 6½-foot window fitted with glass shelves is shaded in summer by a Christmas-berry-tree, *Photinia villosa,* that conveniently drops its leaves in fall to let in full winter sunshine. And rarely is this too strong before March or April, except on very bright snowy days, for petunias or African-violets. Then

Under the long window are cabinets holding decorative pots, saucers, stands, and a hanging basket. *On the shelf,* petunias, impatiens, coleus, and variegated plectranthus make a bright picture. Charles Marden Fitch photo

these are moved back and sheltered by tall geraniums and other sun-lovers.

The casements on the west, protected by storm sash, are also fitted with shelves. At the top a wooden valance conceals the fluorescent tubes there. Because of my preference for vines, I put up brackets and hanging baskets and planters everywhere possible. Below the casements, a plant stand fitted with metal trays for pebbles accommodates ferns and other less sun-demanding plants. The outer front door, with an in-

A lighted closet holds a shelf for fertilizers and sprays, wastebasket, watering can, and cardboards to slip between plants and glass on very cold nights. Charles Marden Fitch photo

The west window of the Plant Room provides adequate light for assorted houseplants, including, *lower left, Philodendron scandens oxycardium; top right,* a *Hedera helix* cultivar in wall bracket; *lower right, Asparagus sprengeri* in a brass pot; *on middle shelf,* fragrant-flowered *Murraya exotica;* and numerous African-violets. Plants on the top shelf receive supplemental light from growth lamps concealed by the valance. George C. Bradbury photo side full-length glass storm door for winter, is kept open except at night and in frigid weather. Screened in summer, the front door admits hours of early eastern sunlight.

Under the long window, cabinets hold equipment and support three 13- by 26-inch metal trays of pebbles inserted in a 16-inch Formica shelf. (These smaller trays are more easily moved for the yearly cleaning

In summer the Plant Room is not entirely denuded. A few ferns, a basket, and a bracket plant, with small new white begonias in white pots, sparsely placed on the pebble trays, make a cool picture in the shade of the Christmas-berry-tree. George Taloumis photo

The Irving Sabos' dining-garden room, measuring 17 by 20 feet, connects the old carriage house and the new dwelling. Sliding glass doors at each end, glass sections in the 11-foot-high roof, and a natural slate floor make this an excellent environment for plants. At this south end a sixteen-year-old balding avocado tree, grown from a pit, supports a climbing citrus in a great ceramic vessel, originally used for the storage of potter's clay and now drilled for drainage. A fuchsia in a basket hangs from the ceiling in winter; in summer it goes outside, suspended in the light open shade of a tree. George Taloumis photo

An old well, protected by an iron cover, is a unique aspect of the Sabo garden room. A copper still with a spigot (from bootlegging days) holds liquid fertilizer for easy dispensing to pots of begonias, chlorophytum, ferns, and philodendron. An angel-wing begonia towers in the background. George Taloumis photo than one long one would be. Plastic trays now generally available could take their place.) Water poured over the pebbles and kept at a level just below the base of the pots provides humidity from 45 to 70, rarely to 80 per cent. Grills conceal radiators, and heat is regulated by a thermostat just for this room, which is kept cooler, especially at night, than the rest of the house. I usually set it at 68 degrees by day, 60 by night, but it gets colder next the glass, of course.

To facilitate care, a small sink was installed in a lighted closet, the space stolen from a big adjacent bedroom closet. This sink makes it easy to wash foliage or spray with an insecticide, though in this cool room protected by a No-Pest Strip, insects rarely appear. Heavy draperies at the living-room doorway and doors elsewhere make it possible to close off this Plant Room, whose fourth side is the stairway. And I cannot tell you what a delight it is every morning, even before coffee, to walk down into my private Eden. In fact, it's not unusual for me to forget morning coffee for half an hour—or longer—while my plants engross me.

As my interests have waxed, expanded, and waned, this Plant Room has been filled with geraniums, African-violets, a collection of fragrant plants, or a grand miscellany of unfamiliar things that I am trying out. A florist plant or two—chrysanthemum, cyclamen, poinsettia—nearly always counts for strong winter color, though in this bright room it is no trick to have flowers on any plants that bloom: African-violets, other gesneriads, geraniums, begonias, impatiens, petunias, as well as vivid leaf tones from coleus, ruellia, variegated ivies, and plectranthus.

My Friends' Plant Rooms

Friends who have built plant rooms report a similar pleasure. My neighbors, the Irving Sabos, have a larger room than mine that also serves as a dining-garden room. It forms a connecting unit between the old carriage house and the new dwelling modeled on French country houses. The walls of the two buildings form the sides, glass panels the ends; glass set into the roof lets in light from above; slates make the flooring. Unique in this garden room is an old well, safely covered by an iron cap, on which plants are set along with a bootlegger's copper still that now holds liquid fertilizer.

With such grand space, big specimens can be accommodated, and to this room have gone certain cherished begonias and stephanotis plants of mine that have outgrown my smaller quarters. A sixteen-year-old avocado, a giant citrus, a hanging fuchsia 4 feet across, uninhibited philodendrons, chlorophytums, and ferns are in scale with these spacious quarters.

In Cazenovia, New York, my architect-sculptor friend, Dorothy Riester, has also built a connector, 12 by 14 feet, between her new "pavilion" and the main house. Through the glass of the south end, the woods are seen. The northern sections look toward the garden. Flagstones in cement delineate a central path that runs between 2-foot-deep beds of soil in which some plants grow directly, particularly the self-sowing impatiens. Thus this indoor Plant Room seems almost a part of the outdoors. Other plants flourish in pots set on top of the earth; giant orange and lemon trees reach toward the skylight, and on one side a pool, shaped from fiberglass, assures humidity.

If you like to *live* with plants rather than *go* to them for brief visits, do consider a way to have a Plant Room. No matter what the architecture of your house, traditional or contemporary, you can probably knock something out as I did or join the old with the new as the Sabos and Riesters have done. There is also the possibility of introducing heat to a cold sun porch and putting glass sections in the roof to get more light in winter. I wouldn't claim any of these possibilities isn't hard on the exchequer but money spent on a Plant Room earns interest of a very satisfactory kind.

18

TROUBLE—WHAT IS IT?

Causes, Controls, Cures Maybe

There is no use making a big to-do about the pests and diseases of houseplants. If you start with healthy specimens—from a reliable mail-order firm or greenhouse or from a friend, whose plants are obviously clean and prospering—and then provide *regular* care and just average know-how, your plants are unlikely to get things. Certainly mine rarely do and they aren't sprayed much—though I admit a monthly spray is good health insurance. However, I find I follow a systematic routine without even realizing it now. And I don't go on pampering "difficult" greenhouse plants, although occasionally I like to try something challenging. Once I find a plant doesn't care for the life style here, I don't mind giving it up. So you may also find that calla-lily begonias, fuchsias, acalypha, achimenes, cape-primrose, gardenias, and some others are not among the most rewarding of indoor plants for you.

Daily Checkup

Let's check again the Seven Keys to Success (Chapter 5), knowing that regular attention transcends all else. Take a wise look at all your plants, preferably in the morning. Don't water them every day unless they need it, and few will. Watering is such a pleasant occupation that I too am inclined to overdo it. But continuously wet soil is most harmful, as is too dry soil, though maybe too dry is the lesser of two evils. Plants in plastic pots need less water than those in clay, and if you have a lot of plants, you will soon discover that certain ones are bellwethers. You won't have to feel the soil in every one every day. When the bellwethers need water they all probably will. Some, like ferns and African-violets, you will try to keep just evenly moist; others, like many of the vines, you can let feel fairly dry before a thorough watering. In any case, no *standing* water in saucers, jardinieres, and especially in decorative pots; put inverted saucers or a block of wood under plants in these, as I do beneath my big begonias and asparagus-ferns.

Pest Deterrence

The well-cared-for healthy plant is not inviting to pests, but sometimes something does show up and you can't imagine why or where it came from. It is good insurance to spray plants about once a month with an insecticide. Aerosols are a great convenience; *just be sure to read the label.* Sometimes a general product will indicate that it is safe for everything but ferns or gardenias and maybe they are just what you had in mind for a cleanup. Malathion 50 is my general favorite in time of need; Kelthane for African-violets.

Many of my friends and I swear by the Shell Chemical Company's No-Pest Strips. These are really pretty ornaments in their gilt containers and they now last for four months. They certainly maintain a pest-free condition in the Plant Room.

One admirer of fuchsias, which are so prone to white fly indoors in winter, claims she couldn't grow them without this Strip control. After trying various other remedies, she saved a beautiful big standard fuchsia that was infested by covering it with a cleaner's plastic bag and hanging the Strip inside. Once the plant was "clean" again, she removed the bag and simply hung the Strip behind a curtain in the same room, with the most satisfactory results. Others who need to "de-pest" smaller plants do the same thing, covering them with plastic food bags, and propping the No-Pest Strip inside.

Like other controls, the No-Pest Strip is out of favor with a great many people because of the vapona gas it emits. Humans don't even smell this but happily it is lethal to our houseplant enemies. Anyway, I use it. I don't give No-Pest Strips to children to play with and I don't hang them in the dining room, kitchen, or bedroom, but I always have one in the

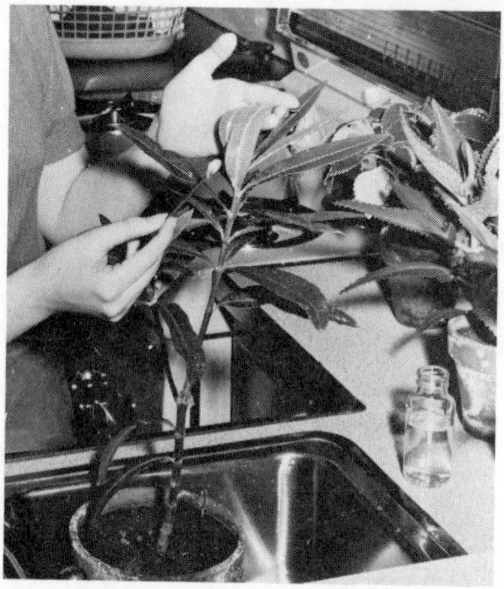

Above. Aerosol sprays are an easy means of controlling or cleaning up insect attacks. Read the label carefully to be sure the formulation is suitable for the plants you wish to spray. (One of my favorite sprays is recommended for African-violets but not for lantanas.) *Below left,* a cotton swab soaked in rubbing alcohol is used to remove mealy bugs from a broad-leaved plant. *Below right,* with pot and surface soil protected by foil, a plant is doused in a malathion solution. Sometimes dipping the whole plant top this way is the only way to clean up a severe attack. U.S.D.A. photos

rather open Plant Room, and to date, my health is perfect. Friends who surreptitiously conceal the Strips in living rooms where plants are grown are also in pretty good shape. All in all we agree that something has got to be left to us to combat what we have to for our plants.

Systemics offer another successful means of pest control, especially for the resistant white fly. Systemics are materials that are drawn into all parts of the plant, which are then lethal to insects that suck or chew leaves or stems. I have found Ortho's Isotox reliable. I sprinkle, according to directions, a heaping teaspoon of the granules over the soil of each pot but, if possible, not touching the stems. Then the soil is thoroughly soaked. With Isotox, you can count on three to four months' protection for your plants. Isotox is particularly helpful if in fall you want to bring plants from the garden to the house. Outdoors a petunia may thrive and bloom well, though alive with white fly; indoors the plant would probably die and certainly it would soon infest others. Application of a systemic can save it for you.

On the following pages, I give a chart on the whole gruesome business of pests and fungus ailments. Throw out the plants whose lost looks are unlikely to be retrieved, try to rescue those that ail but slightly, according to the remedies suggested below.

Trouble		
What It Looks Like	*What It May Be*	*What to Do*
LEAVES		
Browning of tips	Too much or too little water; too much fertilizer; foliage may also be curled due to aphids.	For aphids, strong water spray at sink that reaches underside of leaves; for severe attack, malathion spray or dip (or discard plant); repeat cleanup as condition indicates.
Cottony clusters at leaf joints, also stickiness	Mealy bugs; if sooty mold also, a fungus disease has developed on sticky excreta.	Hand-pick mealy bugs; touch with alcohol-dipped swab; spray with malathion or dip. Discard if diseased.
Defoliation—partial or complete	Sudden temperature drop; draft; reaction to transplanting; or a move to a dim place from sun or to a house from a greenhouse. Overwatering or standing water.	When it occurs, usually too late to remedy. Study the probable cause or causes, and prevent recurrence on this or other plants.
Spotting	Too much water; if ring-spotted, especially African-violets, probably from cold water; burning from sun, especially if foliage is exposed when wet.	As above.
Stickiness	Excreta of aphids (along with curling); of scale (hard, motionless shells, shiny look to foliage); of white flies (along with woolly mold, yellowing of leaves, white cloud of insects if plant is disturbed). (See also cottony clusters.)	Segregate plant. For a light infestation, wash aphids off and hand-pick scale, with attention to underside of leaves; malathion spray or dip, or a suitable aerosol spray at weekly intervals for a heavy attack—or discard.
Yellowing, perhaps with curling, distortion, speckling	Aphids probably. Thrips if streaked, speckled, or blotched and flower buds also damaged.	Treat as for browning of tips above.

TROUBLE

What It Looks Like	*What It May Be*	*What to Do*
WHOLE PLANT		
Crumbly, webbed, grayish look	Spider-mites, notably on English ivy and morning-glory.	Spray top and bottom forcibly at sink to break webs; wash frequently to control. Dimite or Aramite for bad case (or throw out).
Stunted; hard, bunched centers; leaves cupped up or down; stippling along veins or on leaves	Cyclamen or broad mite, particularly on African-violets.	If advanced infestation better throw out plant; at least segregate to prevent spread. Avoid by using sterilized (pasteurized) soil and spraying monthly with Kelthane.
Rotting at base or crown or softening of stems	Excess water settling at crown, not draining down quickly, or fungus disease resulting from wetness.	Cut off and dust soft parts with a fungicidelike sulfur or Fermate; let soil dry out; examine roots; if rotted, cut back, repot in fresh soil, sometimes in a smaller container. Discard if condition is advanced.
Stippling, rusty-brown areas along veins or on leaves	Thrips.	Malathion spray or dip, repeated.

RANDOM THOUGHTS

Orchids to You

For years I have passed orchids by because their out-of-bloom looks do not appeal to me; I mainly select houseplants for year-round beauty and appeal. However, 12,000 enthusiasts (the extent of the American Orchid Society) can hardly be wrong. Orchids *are* fascinating and so in a hesitant way I have begun to grow them, and I am getting hooked, for they are doing well for me. In the photograph of my small fluorescent-light garden you can see that orchids and my saintpaulias are proving good companions. At this stage, I like best the moth orchid, *Phalaenopsis*. When I cut the blooming wands back to the next node after the end flowers fade, it isn't long before twin white "dogwood" blossoms open again. This delights me!

Orchid names are as mind-boggling as those of ferns. The type that grow in trees, the epiphytes (and these are in the majority), come from the grower potted in fir-bark mixtures or chopped tree fern. Orchids with moisture-holding pseudobulbs like Laelias and Cattleyas are permitted to dry between waterings. Epiphytes without pseudobulbs—some Dendrobiums and some Epidendrums—are kept evenly moist but never soaked. About twice a week is right for them and I usually take mine to the kitchen sink and give them a warm-water drench. The orchids potted in soil, the terrestrials, like many Paphiopedilums (Cypripediums), the lady-slipper type, are watered like other houseplants. Also I fog them all frequently as I pass by the light tray, taking care to keep dripping water out of new growth.

Jack Kramer, who raised 100 orchids at windows in a Chicago apartment, once sent me two absolute beauties in my favorite yellow shades—

On a pebble-filled saucer under a Victorian bell jar, a lavender, single ruffled African-violet is a charming companion for a green-and-white dwarf caladium. Charles Marden Fitch photo

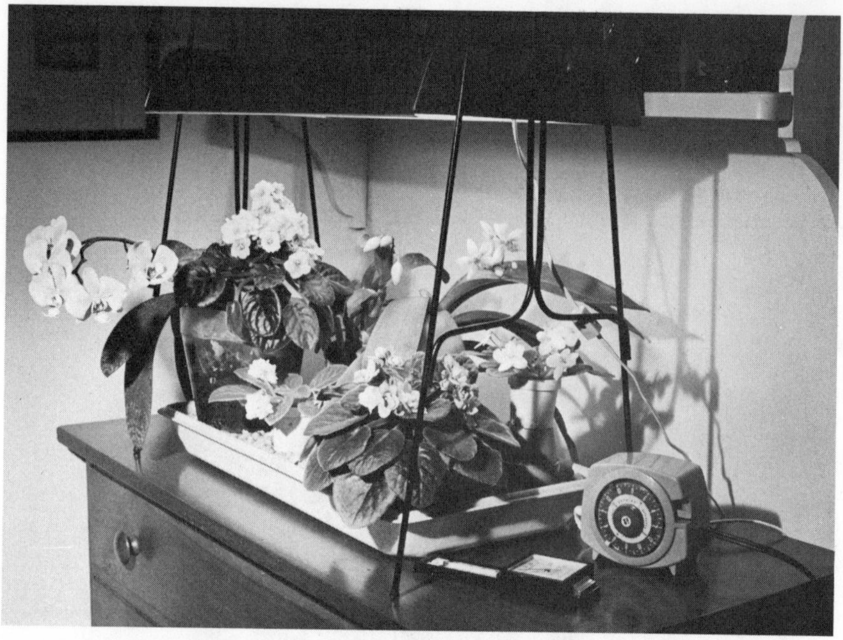

On a pebble-filled tray under a fluorescent-light fixture, warm-preference moth orchids grow with African-violets. At the left, one "violet" sets on the soil of the big orchid pot. A timer on the chest turns lights on and off, and a hygrometer registers heat degrees and humidity per cent. Charles Marden Fitch photo

Dendrobium aggregatum and *D. thyrsiflorum*. They were handsome performers through March and into April but too large, it seemed, for me to accommodate all year so, regretfully, I found a home for them with an orchid-collecting friend who had a small greenhouse. (When I see them blooming handsomely there again in spring, I fear I regret my decision.)

Here is a limited list of orchids that may give you help and satisfaction as it is giving me. Jack and my other orchid-enthusiast friend, Charles Marden Fitch, suggest these for the beginner to enjoy at windows or under lights. They are all "intermediate-to-warm growers" for winter-to-late-spring flowers, since most of us care more for houseplants that bloom then rather than in summer. Only mature or ready-to-bloom *established plants should be purchased*. They do cost the earth—my seven came to $48—but all opened buds at once and some are already repeating. The cheaper collected specimens from the jungle require too much cultural know-how for an orchid novice.

In a 16-inch bubble bowl, Swedish-ivy, full size and the variegated miniature, a white African-violet, a tiny orchid, and an unknown seedling—with a gray-white rock in the center for interest and a ground covering of moss for unity—grow in obvious harmony. Charles Marden Fitch photo

Cattleya hybrids are the "corsage" orchids. These come in almost every color imaginable; there are clear whites, magnificent bronze colors, fire-red, even apple-green ones. Whatever your color preference, buy sturdy seedlings in 3- to 5-inch pots. With minimum care you will have a fine harvest of flowers.

Epidendrum species having pseudobulbs include *E. atropurpureum,* the spring-blooming sprays of green-brown-purple flowers with spicy fragrance, and *E. cochleatum,* a fragrant greenish yellow with a yellow-veined dark purple lip. This blooms through most of the year.

Oncidium ampliatum for late winter into spring, *O. flexuosum* for fall into winter, and *O. splendidum* for spring into summer, all with myriads of yellow flowers, are called dancing ladies or butterfly orchids.

Paphiopedilum (*Cypripedium*) *hirsutissimum* opens waxy, long-lasting, white-striped green flowers, usually spring and fall, above green mottled foliage. *P. maudiae,* a popular hybrid, bears flowers in a delicate harmony of soft green, yellow, and white.

Phalaenopsis hybrids, the moth orchids, especially large whites like 'Elinor Shafer' and 'Mattie Shave,' are handsome with winter and spring flowers that last more than a month. Sometimes they bloom throughout the year if the flowering stems are cut back at nodes. They also come in pink and yellow shades, and bicolors, and delicately spotted ones—the loveliest of all orchids, I think.

Most catalogues from orchid specialists are somewhat terrifying to me, what with my vast ignorance, the enormous number of plants, and the six-syllable nomenclature. If, like me, you are a beginner, I'd suggest you get the *Handbook on Orchid Culture* of the American Orchid Society. It sticks to the bird's-eye view. It costs fifty cents, is free with orders from most growers and to members of the A.O.S. (Order from the Botanical Museum of Harvard University, Cambridge, Mass. 02138.) Then there is *Growing Orchids at Your Windows* by Jack Kramer (Hawthorn Books, Inc., 70 Fifth Ave., New York, N.Y. 10011). This small book has a refreshing simplicity and the beautiful drawings help you get acquainted easily with this very complex family.

These Walls Do Not a Prison Make

If you have never tried growing houseplants, particularly the choice miniature types, in glass enclosures, you have ahead a delightful horticultural adventure. Today apartment dwellers whose space is limited, as well as enthusiasts like me who have plenty of room, are all having fun with our glassed-in gardens. The plants thrive in the humid enclosures as we appreciate the near view and the charming small-scale effect.

Even one plant in a brandy snifter or berry bowl is a delight. On my breakfast table I have a white African-violet in such a bowl, and it is one of the small pleasures of my day. Every morning I am aware of its progress, the abundance of unfolding buds and the shapeliness of the growth.

In summer on the porch the centerpiece for the glass table has been a 12-inch bubble bowl planted with Swedish-ivy—small plants of the standard kind and a variegated miniature that flourished so in its walled setting that it almost lost miniature status; African-violets white and purple; an accommodating miniature orchid, and a pretty volunteer weed with a pointed leaf not yet diagnosed. If you have an old-fashioned bell jar, formerly set over a clock or placed above an arrangement of dried flowers, employ this for a one- or two-plant garden as shown earlier in this chapter with an African-violet and a miniature caladium whose green-and-white leaves offer contrast. (Variegated plants are notably effective in terrarium plantings.)

Or perhaps you have fallen heir, as did my friend Lucy Sargent, to a Wardian case, not the simple glass box of Dr. Ward's original but a handsome piece of parlor furniture, the mahogany of frame and stand ornamented with ormolu mounts. She had just replaced her winter garden with a cool planting of ferns for summer when this picture was taken.

Large glass enclosures like this make it possible to develop Lilliputian landscapes featuring various miniature plants. At a recent African-violet convention in New York, a prize-winning 16-inch bubble bowl portrayed a mountain scene with pebbles simulating a waterfall, and a well-chosen stone a cliff. Wildflower gardens are also possible with small columbines, trilliums, and ferns, collected from the larger plantings on your own place. Even weeds have been known to make an interesting garden under glass. A glass fish tank can also be converted into a terrarium with plantings arranged on several levels and light provided overhead by a fluorescent fixture.

Indeed, almost any glass vessel offers possibilities. You may even want to plant a garden in a narrow-necked bottle. I have watched such demonstrations—the soil poured through a funnel, the plants inserted with special tools—and I know that bottle gardening is not for me. It would drive me up the wall, for it requires infinite patience—and I am somewhat short on that—and very clever fingers indeed. Just wiping off the inside of the glass after planting involves a "special" technique. But the bubble bowls, of which many are now on the market, and terrariums, bought or contrived, and from which the glass can be lifted, make it possible to handle the plantings inside and care for them easily. And you don't have to be a contortionist to do it.

It is not my purpose here to do more than entice you into a delightful aspect of gardening when walls do not a prison make for the plants inside, only an ideal environment. If houseplants have resented the dry air of your dwelling, this way you can offer them something more agreeable. A book like Jack Kramer's *Gardens Under Glass* (Simon and Schuster, 630 Fifth Ave., New York, N.Y. 10019) will tell you ALL; meanwhile here is a brief guidance for a start:

Grow together plants that require about the same conditions—fittonias and begonias are good companions, not cacti and orchids. Use small creepers like babys-tears, selaginella, or moss as groundcover.

To plant, spread a generous layer of coarse gravel or small stones

No longer a utilitarian object, the Wardian case has been transformed here into a handsome piece of furniture for the Victorian parlor, the mahogany of frame and stand ornamented with ormolu mounts. Planting by Lucy Sargent. Charles Marden Fitch photo over the bottom of the container, above this an appropriate soil mixture. The soil may be lighter, more porous than that for potting; a little charcoal added will keep it sweet. In my bubble garden, a third of garden soil, a third humus, and a third perlite worked well, and I'd prefer sand to perlite if I could obtain a small amount. You rarely or never have to feed or water an enclosed planting.

A pane of glass over the opening keeps the moisture in. If the glass gets misted, remove and wipe it, and don't replace for half an hour or so. You will find that some species, among them African-violets and other gesneriads, do better if a small area is left open or the top is without cover as with brandy snifters.

Set your glass garden safely in a fully light place, in sunlight only if plants seem to require it, but sun through glass may burn. My small violet on the breakfast table gets only an hour or so of early sunlight. Geraniums need the sun and a wide-mouthed, open glass house, for they do not require high humidity; roses like the sun but a closed house.

Herbs in Winter

If you are a good cook who depends all summer on your outdoor herb patch for seasonings, you will also want some pots of herbs indoors in winter. You can grow these along with other plants in any bright place in the house, but the ideal spot is, of course, right in the kitchen, and a corner facing east is ideal, south if the location is not too hot. Except in the dead of winter when no sun is strong, about three hours of sunlight, say 10 A.M. to 1 P.M., is fine. However, hot sun through glass and a dry atmosphere spell death. A deep round tray covered with gravel, pebbles, or perlite and set on a Lazy Susan makes an excellent base for a pretty and convenient winter herb garden. You can turn the Lazy Susan instead of the individual pots and so easily give the plants equal exposure, preventing the spindly growth that results when plants reach for the light in one direction only.

Lacking a *bright* window, what pleasure you can have with a fluorescent light setup installed under a kitchen cabinet and over a counter, perhaps near the chopping block where you prepare salads, but in any case *not* next the stove. Or you may want a table-top unit like mine for the kitchen or elsewhere. The 2- by 4-foot tray of pebbles beneath the lights accommodates some ten 3-inch pots or six to eight 4's. Clay pots seem to suit herbs better than plastic ones, and growth lamps like Gro-Lux apparently have an advantage over the commercial type.

Less than a dozen different herbs make an excellent indoor culinary garden and whether you grow more than one pot of each depends on your space. Perhaps you will order all your plants early in fall from an herb specialist. Certainly you don't want to pot from the garden and bring in big specimens, for they won't succeed. (In fact, few plants will accept root restriction and indoor conditions at the same time with equanimity.) However, *potted* herbs of suitable size can be transferred successfully from outdoors with due regard for humidity and fresh air at the start.

If you want to grow your own plants, sow seed of the annuals in spring in pots sunk in the ground. By fall the thinned-out plants will be of suitable size. With the perennials, take cuttings in spring or pot up small divisions from your big plants then, except the tender rosemary. Always pot- or tub-grown, this is wintered on a sunny, unheated, but not freezing porch or in front of a window in an old-fashioned cold pantry.

Now what culinary herbs are the most useful, and also most likely to prosper indoors? The annuals, like curly basil—easier than sweet basil—dill and marjoram are grown from seed, as are parsley—both the curly and the Italian—and French tarragon. Clumps of chives, potted and brought in after the first freeze, are cut daily, the extra clippings frozen in small plastic envelopes for use as needed. Orégano, sage, spearmint (this thrives in the shade of other plants), thyme, and winter savory are best grown from spring cuttings or small potted root divisions of your garden plants. You probably won't want both orégano—which will flourish handsomely in a hanging container suspended above your window-sill plants—and sweet marjoram since the two serve much the same flavorsome purpose, and cuttings of orégano are more likely to thrive indoors than seedlings of marjoram.

I suppose we all want parsley, maybe two pots of it, since we snip this for decoration as well as flavoring. Then we need chives, cut fine and often for soups, salads, cream-cheese hors d'oeuvre, and so on. Curly basil goes with tomatoes and spaghetti sauce; pinch out the tops regularly so seed won't form and the plant will renew itself in a week. Cut the top leaves of orégano to insure bushy growth. Winter savory, a pleasing sprawler, looks nice on the outside of the tray. Sprigs of it greatly improve green beans. Cut sweet marjoram frequently to prevent blossoming; it's good in cream soups and for egg dishes. Get a pot of garden or English thyme for stuffings and to season roasts of pork or lamb, and one of the mints—spearmint, *Mentha spicata,* is best—for mint sauce for lamb. Sage may also be for you; I can't bear it but many

Spearmint from spring cuttings thrives in the kitchen herb garden.
Merry Gardens photo

like it, especially in turkey dressing. Only use fresh sage sparingly, for it can have a surprising laxative effect.

Herbs are satisfactory indoor plants provided they don't dry out and don't get too hot. Humidity from cooking and dishwashing promotes health but misting two or three times a week is almost essential. Daily checking of soil is important though not necessarily daily watering. However, take care, for herbs are plants that do not readily recover from drought. But wetness is anathema; with proper drainage this is an unlikely hazard. Keep in mind the need for fresh air for herbs as well as humans but admit it indirectly in cold weather. When it is very cold, slip cardboard or newspaper between plants and glass at night, rarely through the day as well.

Herbs thrive in a mixture of roughly three parts garden soil and two parts sand or perlite. Bought from a reliable source, plants will probably be potted in 2½'s. You may have to repot in the course of the winter. When you do it is essential to add some lime, a teaspoonful to a 5-inch pot of soil mixture, for most herbs don't thrive on acidity. By all means take care to provide good drainage; a soggy soil condition assures a quick demise.

Frequent fertilizing is not necessary for herbs. About twice a month, apply a liquid fertilizer at half the recommended strength. Keep plants free of pests by spraying with a weak solution of some mild detergent like Ivory Liquid and tepid water. Be sure to reach the underside of foliage, especially of such leafy growers as orégano.

From the Kitchen

The kitchen offers some delightful houseplants, notably the AVOCADO, whose admirers are legion. I realized this anew when I had my last "complete" physical examination. As the doctor punched, prodded, and peered, he diverted me with an account of his family's enthusiasm for the avocado. "Four trees, 3 to 4 feet, and all different, no trouble at all, quite a grove," he told me.

Another avocado enthusiast, my friend Harriet Kenney, uses the trees as background for an indoor garden, the tubs in a sunken bed at the right of the front door. Each of the trees has a history. Seventeen-year-old daughter Erin's dates back to show-and-tell days in kindergarten; son Peter's, newly planted, measures just 14 inches; the largest, a 5-foot fifteen-year-old tree with multiple branches, now growing in a 20- by 20-inch redwood planter, is a memorial to an old friend. (This tree suffered devastation when a neighbor's parakeet, a summer boarder, developed a taste for the leaves, but the avocado leafed out again.) It requires two gallons of water every other day and fertilizer every other week. Mrs. Kenney applied a fish emulsion until the family rebelled for the obvious reason; now she uses Hyponex.

If you want to grow an avocado tree, select a ripe fruit and remove the pulp. The seed or pit should show signs of cracking and may even have a little sprout or two. If it looks quite hard, wait for another salad to give you the seed in a more likely stage. For growing I prefer my hyacinth glass with the cupped top; in this the seed is supported as water reaches the base. Time-honored is the three-toothpick method.

In a home setting, an avocado, grown from a seed, makes a tall handsome tree in the third year. The Rex begonia beside it offers an interesting contrast in form. Jack Roche photo

Thrust these toothpicks into the sides of the seed to support it on the edge of a glass of water, and keep the water level just up to the seed; don't float it or it will rot.

You might start this business in December. Roots will appear in two weeks or so and top growth about the same time. When you see strong root growth in February, transfer the avocado to a 4-inch pot of average soil and, once it gets going, pinch out the top to make it bushy. By early summer you will have a nice little tree, 12 to 14 inches high, depending on how much you have checked the upward surge in favor of branching. Of course, children delight in the whole avocado venture.

And had you thought of a SWEET-POTATO vine? Framing a window garden with the pretty foliage (it is an *Ipomoea* like the morning-glory) is an easy almost no-cost way to a leafy kitchen bower. Today the tubers are treated to retard sprouting but under proper encouragement the chemical soon wears off. Wash, don't scrub, the potato and set it in a narrow-neck vase or a mason jar, or select a pair of vases, glass or ceramic, for a balanced treatment. Place the tuber, root end down, so that no more than half of it reaches the water, and be sure to maintain this water level. Evaporation can be fast and drying out is fatal.

In the course of ten days in a cool dark place, roots will form. Then move the potato to a light or sunny window, where sprouts will soon be in evidence—in all, three to four weeks after "planting." Don't let all those little spikes develop or you will have chaos, not a vine. Pinch out all but two or three, then train the leaf strands on strong cord. (Cup hooks are one means of supporting the string if the stretch is long.) The vine will grow fast up and then across the top where it can meet its partner if you have another vine coming up the other side.

CARROT TOPS will make a pretty table centerpiece with a ferny look if 1-inch top sections of root, the stems cut back, are arranged in a low bowl of pebbles with water. Children enjoy this too, for it doesn't take long for the carrots to sprout. Place four or five tops in a low bowl; maintain a water level up to, but not high enough to submerge, the sections. Set the bowl in a light place, where little green shoots will soon push out and the decorative feathery tops develop.

I have also grown beet tops and horseradish but in 3- to 5-inch pots of sandy soil (or perlite). Either vegetable makes handsome foliage, the beets with red tones in the leaves, the horseradish all green, the silhouette effective. A pair of either in my gilded containers make attractive window plants and, of course, puzzle friends who are familiar with foliage plants but hardly expect vegetables in the living room.

GARDEN SHRUBS OPEN WINTER FLOWERS

A vase of glowing golden forsythia in January—still the dead of winter only the shrubs don't seem to care, for the sap is rising—is a lovely sight set among green houseplants. And there are many other common garden shrubs that can be as easily forced, such as the winter-honeysuckle, whose tiny bloom will so deliciously perfume a whole room. Wait for one of those unexpectedly almost warm winter days; then go forth with your sharp pruners and gather bouquets which at this stage appear to be only a bunch of brushwood. However, the blossoms are there just waiting for the warmth and light your windows can supply. Choose branches—some long, some short, some straight, some curved—but particularly with many little bumps (flower and leaf buds) along their lengths.

Indoors, cut your material to attractive bouquet lengths; then mash the ends with a hammer and fill your vase with warm water. My forsythia goes in the sun on the living-room window sill. After the branches are in full bloom, I move the vase to the cold garage to prolong freshness.

Here is a chart of delightful possibilities of flower and foliage with suggestions for timing. Of course, you can cut and force later but I always like to cut as early as possible. You will find that the nearer you gather to the natural leafing and blooming time the fewer the weeks for forcing. These are just a few of the possibilities. You could also bring in magnolia, rhododendron, mountain-laurel, and wisteria in March but they usually take five or six weeks to open, and this hardly seems worth while so near the time of color in the outdoor garden.

Plant	When to Cut	Forcing Time
Forsythia	Mid-January	3 weeks
Honeysuckle-bush	Mid-January	2
Flowering Cherry	Early February	2–4
Flowering Quince	Mid-February	4
Willow	February (any time)	2
Red Maple	Late February	2
Flowering Crabapple and Apple	Mid-March	2–3
Flowering Dogwood	Mid-March	3

Flowers All the Time

If you want constant bloom in your indoor garden, that is exactly what you can have, provided, of course, you have a fully light or a sunny window. Possibilities are limitless and, with only a modicum of planning, various houseplants will be in flower through the year. During the gray weeks of January, budding will be less exuberant but still there will be color. Since I have an outdoor garden, I do not plan for June to September inside, but if you live in an apartment without a balcony, you can have color indoors even in summer with achimenes, African-violets, fuchsias, lipstick-vine, gloxinias, and wax begonias set among your green ferns and vines, and caladiums and "Firebird" coleus for bright foliage accents.

Standbys for Continuous Bloom

African-violet
Baby Cyclamen
Begonias, Wax
Crown-of-Thorns
Impatiens
Trailing Velvet-plant

October–November

African-violet
Begonias, Wax
Bouvardia
Campanulas
Chrysanthemum (florist)
Clerodendrum
Geranium
Impatiens
Jasmines (true and so-called)
Nasturtium (long cuttings)
Plumbago capensis
Sweet-olive
Thanksgiving Cactus

Bulbs: French-Roman Hyacinths, Paperwhite Narcissus —for Thanksgiving

December

African-violet
Begonias, Wax
Bouvardia
Christmas-cactus (florist)
Crown-of-Thorns
Cyclamen (florist)
Geranium
Impatiens
Kalanchoe
Poinsettia (florist)
Sweet-olive

Fruit: Ardesia, Christmas-Pepper, Jerusalem-cherry, Otaheite-Orange

Bulbs: Amaryllis, Calla-lily (white), French-Roman Hyacinths, Paperwhite Narcissus —for Christmas

January

African-violet
Baby Cyclamen (off and on through year)
Begonias, Wax, many others
Bouvardia
Crown-of-Thorns
Cyclamen
Egyptian Star-cluster (off and on through year)
Gardenia (with luck in June)
Geranium
German-violet
Jasmines (true and so-called)
Marica
Petunias (from garden plans)
Plumbago capensis (to April)
Sweet-olive
Trailing Velvet-plant (most of year)
Yesterday-Today-and-Tomorrow (to July)
Fruit: Ardisia
Citrus
Jerusalem-cherry
Bulbs: Paperwhite Narcissus
French-Roman Hyacinths
Forced Branches: Forsythia, Honeysuckle-bush

February–March

African-violet
Apostle-plant
Azalea (florist or your own)
Begonias, Wax, others
Blue-sage
Bouvardia
Citrus
Crown-of-Thorns
Cyclamen
Geranium
'Heavenly-Blue' Morning-Glory (from seed)
Iboza riparia
Impatiens
Jasmines (true and so-called)
Lily-of-the-Valley (forced pips)
Petunias
Poinsettia
Roses (miniature)
Strawberry-geranium
Swedish-ivy
Sweet-olive
Wax-plant

Bulbs: Amazon-lily
Aztec-lily
Ginger-lily
Forced Branches: Flowering Cherry, Crabapple, Dogwood, Quince

April–May

African-violet
Begonias, Wax, others
Black-eyed-Susan vine (from seed)
Crown-of-Thorns
Cyclamen
Easter Lily (florist)
Gardenia
Geranium
Gloxinia
Impatiens
Jasmines (true and so-called)
Passion-flower
Petunia
Poinsettia
Plumbago capensis
Stephanotis
Sweet-olive
Bulbs: Calla-lily (golden)
Gloriosa-lily (to October)
Polyanthus Narcissus

Do Plants Have Feelings Too?

Perhaps you are concerned about the emotional needs of your plants. Do you talk to them? Do you play music for them? Do you protect them from psychological shock?

I always thought enthusiasts who talked this way, and claimed success accordingly, were simply knowledgeable and sensitive to the needs of their plants. I thought the claim for emotions in plants was ridiculous. These conclusions predated my exposure to a lecture by Cleve Backster, who is not a horticulturist but a specialist in the use of polygraph machines—lie-detectors—and he came upon certain plant reactions incidentally in his work on human reactions. As the *Wall Street Journal* reported:

"His experiments, in fact, seem to indicate that besides some sort of telepathic communication system plants also possess something closely akin to feelings or emotions. . . . They appreciate being watered. They worry when a dog comes near. They faint when violence threatens their own well-being. And they sympathize when harm comes to animals and insects close to them.

"Mr. Backster got hooked on plant studies Feb. 2, 1966, in the interrogation room of the Backster School here where he trains private investigators, police and government personnel to use polygraph machines—lie-detectors. He wondered how long it would take water he had just given a tall, droopy-leaved dracaena plant to travel from the roots to the leaves, so he connected a pair of polygraph electrodes to a leaf, figuring that the moisture might gradually change its resistance level enough to register on his lie-detector.

"To his surprise, he got an immediate polygraph reaction pattern that closely resembled that of a person under emotional stimulation. Wondering whether the plant would also produce a reaction similar to a human's if its safety was threatened, Mr. Backster decided to try burning a leaf. But before he could reach for a match, 'at the split second that I had the image of fire in my mind, the recording pen bounced right off the top of the chart,' he recalls. 'It really shook me up.' "

He claims that a vegetable can "faint" when threatened with boiling water, that plants even have memories. "Six students draw lots to see who will uproot and tear to shreds one of two plants alone in a room. Later, the surviving plant shows no reaction when five of the students re-enter the room, one by one, but it faints when the plant killer returns."

Mr. Backster's report seemed to me astoundingly credible, although his speculations have not caused me to treat my houseplants any differently than before I heard him. He himself, not being a trained horticulturist, makes no definite claims; he simply offers his experimental results to those working in other disciplines: botany, plant research, and so forth. It will be interesting to hear about the findings from the carefully controlled experiments now under way.

WHAT TO DO WHEN

Some month-by-month suggestions to keep your houseplants beautiful—and interesting

January

Houseplants sense the turn of the year, the welcome lengthening hours of daylight. Vines grow faster now, ferns thrust up new fronds, geraniums bud more freely. You discover that more water is taken up and the response to fertilizer is gratifying. Remember to ventilate; there are always some quite warm days this month.

AMARYLLIS. Cut back the faded flower stalks but treat this as the fine, strap-leaved foliage plant it is—plenty of water and plant food.

BROAD-LEAVED FOLIAGE PLANTS. As your strength returns after the holidays, go over rubber-plants, dracaenas, wax-plants, and others with a soft soapy cloth, then with just a wet cloth to remove the suds. With pores freed of dust, they will look and feel much better.

CHRISTMAS-CACTUS. If it hasn't bloomed yet—it can't always be timed—give it full sun, fertilizer, but not too much water; this one may need it only every third day.

CYCLAMEN. Assure five to six months of bloom by growing it *cold* with soil evenly damp. It will take a lot of water. Even at a north window, it will open every one of those maybe fifty buds.

GERANIUMS. Move the big rested plants, which you potted from the garden and have been growing quite cold, to full sun and warmth, but best not above 65 degrees if you can manage it. Water more freely and fertilize as you see the plants responding.

GINGER-LILY. Pot a tuber of *Kaempferia rotunda* now for March-to-April bloom.

MORNING-GLORIES AND BLACK-EYED-SUSAN VINES. Sow seeds the first day of the New Year. In exactly eight weeks you will have flowers on your 'Heavenly Blue' plants; in eleven to twelve weeks the Susans will be dotted with bright yellow blooms.

POINSETTIA. To insure months of beauty, take care to remove any little shoots that may push out below the colorful bracts.

SHRUB BOUQUETS. Cut some forsythia branches now, mash ends, arrange in a vase, and set in a sunny window for colorful winter bloom.

February

Everything will be burgeoning now as the sun is stronger. Plants that have been biding their time, like the geraniums you started in September, will start to bud, the jasmines will open their fragrant flowers. The window garden will grow more and more colorful.

ASPARAGUS-FERN. Protect from too much heat and sun; if long old branches turn yellow, cut them off at the soil line.

BEGONIAS, WAX. If these get leggy, cut back some of the stems in each pot. As these grow tall, cut back others and you will maintain bushy growth.

CHRISTMAS-CACTUS. When bloom is finished, grow this somewhat dry and prune off a link or two for shapeliness.

CYCLAMEN. As some flowers fade and some leaves discolor, yank both out from the base of the plant.

GLORIOSA-LILY. Pot this delightful climber early this month for spring and summer bloom.

KALANCHOE. Keep a careful watch for mealy bug; it loves this plant. Clean it off with an alcohol-dipped swab, then give a clear water spray.

MARICA. Don't cut off the faded flowers unless you don't want more plants. If little plants develop at the ends of long stems, and bloom there, put pots of soil under them so they will root and make more maricas to give away.

ORANGE AND LEMON TREES. Give warmer locations, up to 65 degrees; as spring gets nearer, they will burst into fragrant bloom.

SHRUBS TO FORCE. Branches of flowering quince and cherry will bloom in a vase indoors, and the weeping willow will produce graceful greenery.

March

With your good care, some plants will definitely have outgrown their locations. It's too soon to put them outdoors but your local library or hospital will be grateful for your decorative houseplants. Stick in the soil a big plant label with name and a few vital instructions; this will be much appreciated and insure longer life for these growing things.

AFRICAN-VIOLETS. As the early spring sunshine gets stronger, move these out of direct sun but keep in full light. Turn them at the window. Here or under fluorescent lights, they will be covered with bloom. Don't be tempted to repot; even quite large plants are adequately provided for in 3's or 4's. Fertilize freely.

FRAGRANT PLANTS. Try to buy a stephanotis now, more likely from a florist than by mail order. It will delight you for years to come. Other scented plants for this season when your window garden should smell delicious are the star-jasmines, *Trachelospermum.*

GARDENIA. Try to grow this greenhouse subject cool, 60 degrees daytime; it may tolerate 70 degrees but then watch out for mealy bugs and red-spider. If you have successfully brought this through winter and it is now covered with fat, but very slow, buds, shower tops weekly, daily is better, and maybe "tent" the plant for a few weeks with a perforated plastic bag. To maintain acidity, water with a vinegar solution—½ teaspoon to 1 quart of water—or fertilizer with Miracid. From now on water even more freely and each week set the pot in a pail of water to drink its fill.

IVY. Watch now for aphids that may attack the winter-weary plants. Strong syringing at the sink will deter them.

LILY-OF-THE-VALLEY. Ask your florist now for cold-storage forcing pips. In twenty-one days they will bring a lovely fragrance to your rooms.

April

Keep doors and windows open as much as weather permits and cleanse leafy tops frequently. But avoid chilling and never set your tender plants out for a "refreshing" shower; more likely, they will catch cold. If strong sunlight is wilting foliage, slat the blinds or draw a curtain.

AFRICAN-VIOLETS. If plants are getting long-necked, remove them from the pots, slice off some of the lowest roots and try to return to the same pots, setting plants low enough in the soil to cover the bare necks.

CYCLAMEN. If the last buds have opened, retire this plant to any cool, out-of-sight place but water often enough to let the corm mature properly and not die of drought.

FERNS. They will seem quite frantic with new fronds. Water freely but don't let the pots in decorative jardinieres stand in water. Watch out for scale.

GERANIUMS. Prune judiciously to encourage low, stocky growth, but don't cut back so hard you remove a lot of flowering wood.

May

Plants are growing fast these spring days and so require plenty of food, water, and fresh air. Watch for signs of trouble after the long indoor winter, and syringe tops frequently. Get after any infestation promptly; many plants are somewhat tired now and not in shape to cope with pests. You could begin to discard!

AZALEA. Repot late this month or early next in rich acid soil. Return to the same low pot if possible. Feed regularly through the summer except during hot weeks.

SPIDER-PLANT. For more of these, cut off and pot the new little plantlets dangling at the ends of pendant leaves or stems.

STRAWBERRY-BEGONIA. You can also detach the young replicas hanging threadlike from the big plant. In small separate pots, they will grow fast.

WAX-PLANT. Should you be lucky enough to have old plants that bloom, take care not to cut the flower stems; these are the source of next year's flowers.

June

As soon as frost is unlikely—I wait until after Memorial Day—take all the houseplants outside for a thorough examination (don't be afraid to throw away any that are ailing). Recondition the others. Many will need pots one size larger. Big plants will thrive without repotting but a replacement of topsoil with a rich fresh mixture will revitalize them. Hose the tops of all of plants and select proper summer quarters outdoors or on porch or terrace.

GERANIUMS, ZONAL. Early this month take cuttings for next October's bloom. Insert in pockets of sand in 3-inch pots of houseplant soil.

IVY. Hang baskets in a light place with only a few hours of preferably morning sun.

POINSETTIA. Remove and pot separately the ferns that came along with this gift plant. Cut back poinsettia tops to 3 inches; repot in fresh soil but in the same pots if possible. Water and feed regularly through summer. Pinch back often to promote low bushy growth.

PORCH PLANTS. Make your porch or terrace a bower with your vines and trailing plants in pretty pots suspended from birdcage hangers.

July

Both you and the houseplants, now outdoors, can take it easy through the heat and humidity. Just remember to water all the plants, the outdoor ones when there is little rainfall, the porch plants as usual. During extreme heat and humidity, don't fertilize unless urgent growth indicates the need. Some plants resent high humidity, as do geraniums and African-violets, which may be mite-inclined in the unfavorable atmosphere. Bring these back to the pebble trays indoors.

August

As the summer ends, begin to plan the window garden; order some new plants soon. Do try a few unfamiliar ones, perhaps a miniature cyclamen, pentas, blue-sage, fragrant jasmines. Count on African-violets, wax begonias, and impatiens plants for steady bloom.

AMARYLLIS. Late this month stop fertilizing and water less. When leaves are somewhat yellowed and getting dry, cut back to 2 to 3 inches. Bring indoors, store in a cool place for six to eight weeks, watering about every third week.

CALLA-LILY. Pot bulbs of the white ones early this month for Christmas bloom.

CYCLAMEN. When sprouts appear on your resting plant, clean off the top growth and reset the corm so it protrudes about ½ inch above the soil.

GERANIUMS, ZONAL. Take cuttings now to grow on for February bloom. Shift the rooted spring cuttings to 3-inch pots.

IVY, ENGLISH. Take cuttings, long and short, from your outdoor plants, to grow indoors in vases of water—useful for arrangements with a few flowers. Remove below-water leaves and take more pieces than you think you will need; older branches don't always root. Twelve-inch clusters are the best. Keep vases on the porch until next month's bring-in of the houseplants.

PACHYSANDRA. Pull up some rooted sections or take cuttings from outdoor groundcover areas. Insert in a strong pinholder in a low bowl for a table centerpiece. Plants will grow; cuttings will root.

PLUMBAGO CAPENSIS. Late this month thin out the tops a little and cut back a few inches to reduce the rampant summer growth to room size.

September

Before nights get cold and there is even a light frost, houseplants should come in and be gradually acclimated to house conditions. Right after Labor Day, I move the outdoor ones to the porch where there is less light than in the open and they stay there for a couple of weeks. Before coming in, pots should be scrubbed, tops cleansed with a thorough water syringing, and then given a good insecticide spraying so they will be in a good clean condition and no pest epidemics will start. In my experience, House and Garden Raid, Ortho, and Pratt are safe and convenient aerosols for most houseplants, but read the label. Hang a No-Pest Strip among your plants for continued control of insects. Indoors, keep windows open for hours daily to give plenty of fresh air through the first weeks. Then there should be a minimum of leaf drop and general dissatisfaction with the home environment. Avoid high heat, syringe tops frequently.

ANNUALS FROM THE GARDEN. Do pot lantanas, petunias, impatiens, wax begonias used for bedding, marigolds, if you have dwarf types, and marguerites for colorful indoor bloom through the whole winter. Trim them back a little for shapeliness but try to pick bushy growers that won't need much shaping. Set the newly potted plants on the shaded porch steps and fog tops often for seven to ten days while plants acclimate themselves before being brought to the porch.

FRENCH-ROMAN HYACINTHS. Early this month, arrange bulbs in bowls of pebbles and water and set in a cold, not freezing, place for five to six weeks of rooting. (Allow ten weeks in all.)

GERANIUMS. Take cuttings of window-box and garden plants. Young plants will bloom about February. If you pot up the big ones, trim back tops to three stems, 3 inches long. Arrange for a dim cold rest (45 to 50 degrees) and water only about once a week or less. The old plants will be unlikely to bloom before January. Cuttings of the scenteds—rose, lemon, mint—root quickly in water and make a nice winter bouquet.

JASMINES. Prune back and trim out dead wood to make shapely plants but cut as little as possible, for these are now starting to bloom. Grow them cool.

PAPERWHITE NARCISSUS. For Thanksgiving bloom, start mid-month right in the living room, unless you keep that room very warm. (Allow about ten weeks for these early plantings.)

SUPPLIES. If you have compost in the garden, put a goodly supply through a ½-inch sieve for winter needs. If nematodes are rampant where you live, pasteurize the soil.

October

Be sure to order a choice tender bulb or two to highlight your indoor window gardens—an Amazon-, gloriosa-, or Jacobean-lily, perhaps a few callas. Be mindful of ventilation these warm fall weeks; keep windows open for hours each day. When it turns cold, ventilate more cautiously, but regularly from an adjoining hall or room.

AFRICAN-VIOLETS. Place them in full sun as days grow shorter toward the end of the month.

BEGONIAS, WAX. If your garden supplied none, buy plants of these for steady bloom at light or sunny windows.

CALLA-LILIES. Pot the pink ones now for three weeks of winter bloom.

CHRISTMAS-CACTUS. Set the plant in a cold dim place and do not water *for the entire month.*

FRENCH-ROMAN HYACINTHS. After five or six weeks of cold rooting, bring bowls to a cool, sunny window for Thanksgiving bloom that will continue for about three weeks. For Christmas bloom, start mid-October.

ORANGE AND LEMON TREES. Grow these cold and on the dry side for the next few months.

POINSETTIA. To get Christmas bloom, give these short-day plants at least twelve hours of certain darkness for seventy days. I move mine to a closet 8 P.M. to 8 A.M.

November

This is a dull month. Plants requiring a great deal of sun, like the geranium, will not bloom freely except under fluorescent light, but the African-violets, impatiens plants, and wax begonias will be full of color despite sunless days. Withhold fertilizer through weeks of dark weather from plants that seem slow and reluctant to bloom. Watch for stickiness on leaves or on plant shelves. Soap and water will clean up a mild attack of aphids or scale; resort to malathion if infestation is heavy or spray repeatedly with a houseplant aerosol.

AFRICAN-VIOLETS. Turn plants a quarter each week to keep them shapely. Place a collar made from a cut-out paper plate under the leaves of a droopy plant. It will help to raise and flatten out the foliage again.

AMARYLLIS. Treat yourself to an already potted Dutch hybrid. To start with, grow it warm (70 to 75 degrees) in rather a dim spot, water sparingly until growth is about 6 inches along; then move to a cooler sunny place.

CALLA-LILY. Pot the yellow ones now for Easter bloom; allow about four months.

CHRISTMAS-CACTUS. Water only twice, once early, once mid-month. At the end of the month, move to a sunny window, water weekly at first, then every other day with fertilizer solution as for other plants.

IVY, ENGLISH. Douse the bouquets frequently at the sink to avoid attacks of aphids.

KALANCHOE. For Christmas bloom, provide twelve to fourteen hours of darkness for three weeks before Christmas. I put this short-day plant in the dark closet along with the poinsettia.

December

Take care of the lovely florist plants you receive this month. Avoid drafts, high heat, and low humidity. *Remove foil wrappings immediately;* they are death traps. Before you get too holiday-busy, give your permanent plants a good showering. Polish windowpanes and glass shelves. Perhaps arrange a Christmas picture, as I do, with a madonna figure and tall candles set among the greens. Guests and passers-by will enjoy the small drama.

AMARYLLIS. Move to a sunny east window at about 65 to 70 degrees.

AZALEA. Grow it cool, below 60 degrees if possible, and be most careful not to let soil dry out. Once a week water by the pot-submergence method and spray tops at the sink. Fertilize with an acid plant food or keep soil acidified by watering with a solution of ½ teaspoon vinegar in 1 quart of water. An east or west window with moderate sun is fine now. Nip off faded flowers.

CYCLAMEN. No question about it, this must be grown not cool but cold for the great crop of buds to open and not dry up. *Keep the soil wet* and give a cool place in full light, cold to 45 degrees at night.

KALANCHOE. Put this gift plant in a sunny window to get repeated bloom; it won't mind 70 degrees by day, but 60 to 65 by night is better, and it doesn't require high humidity. Watch out for mealy bugs.

POINSETTIA. This should last for several months at least. Place it at a cool window or, if your living room is fairly warm, move it to a cooler place at night.

WHERE TO BUY

Here is a list of growers and suppliers by no means complete, but all reliable, their stimulating catalogues grand reading. You can also obtain some pesticides (aerosols), fertilizers, and packaged soils from your local hardware stores and garden centers.

Alberts & Merkel Bros., Box 637, Boynton Beach, Florida 33435. Orchids, other tropicals; catalogue 50¢.

Black Magic Products, 421 N. Altadena Drive, Pasadena, California 91107. Soils and fertilizers; free catalogue.

Buell's Greenhouses, Eastford, Connecticut 06242. Specialist: African-violets, gloxinias, other gesneriads; catalogue $1.00.

W. Atlee Burpee Co., Box 6929, Philadelphia, Pennsylvania 19132. Bulbs, plants, seed; free catalogue.

The Conard-Pyle Co., Star Roses, West Grove, Pennsylvania 19390. Miniature roses; free catalogue.

P. deJager & Sons, Inc., 188 Asbury Street, South Hamilton, Massachusetts 01982. Bulbs; free catalogue.

Edelweiss Gardens, 54 Robbinsville-Allentown Road, Robbinsville, New Jersey 08691. Houseplants; catalogue 35¢.

Fischer Greenhouses, Linwood, New Jersey 08221. African-violets, soils, supplies; catalogue 25¢.

Bernard D. Greeson, 3548 N. Cramer Street, Shorewood, Wisconsin 53211. Fluorescent equipment, soils, sprays, dusts, supplies in small quantities; list 10¢.

The Houseplant Corner, Box 810, Oxford, Maryland 21654. Fluorescent equipment, houseplant supplies; catalogue 20¢.

Margaret Ilgenfritz Orchids, Box 665, Monroe, Michigan 48161. Orchids; catalogue $1.00.

Kartuz Greenhouses, 92 Chestnut Street, Wilmington, Massachusetts 01887. Specialist: gesneriads, exotics; catalogue 50¢.

Logee's Greenhouses, 55 North Street, Danielson, Connecticut 06239. Specialist: begonias, geraniums, rare plants; catalogue $1.00.

Lyndon Lyon, 14 Mutchler Street, Dolgeville, New York 13329. African-violets, miniatures, trailers; miniature roses; free catalogue.

Rod McLellan Co., 1450 El Camino Real, So. San Francisco, California 94080. Orchids, cork bark; free catalogue.

Merry Gardens, Camden, Maine 04843. Specialist: begonias, geraniums, vines, rare plants; catalogue 50¢.

Geo. W. Park Seed Co., Inc., Greenwood, South Carolina 29646. Bulbs, some houseplants, seeds, supplies; free catalogue.

Plant Marvel Laboratories, 624 W. 119th Street, Chicago, Illinois 60628. Water-soluble plant foods, aerosol insecticides, supplies; free catalogue.

Road Runner Ranch, 2458 Catalina Avenue, Vista, California 92083. Specialist: geraniums; free catalogue.

Roehrs Exotic Nurseries, East Rutherford, New Jersey 07073. Houseplants, great variety; catalogue 10¢, prefer greenhouse visit.

Tinari Greenhouses, 2325 Valley Road, Huntingdon Valley, Pennsylvania 19006. Specialist: African-violets, also supplies, equipment; free catalogue.

Tropical Paradise Greenhouse, 8825 West 79th Street, Overland Park, Kansas 66204. Houseplants, supplies.

Tube Craft, Inc., 1311 W. 80th street, Cleveland, Ohio 44102. Fluorescent equipment; free catalogue.

Van Bourgondien's, Box A, 245 Farmingdale Road, Route 109, Babylon, New York 11702. Bulbs, corms, and tubers; free catalogue.

Wilson Bros., Roachdale, Indiana 46172. Specialist: geraniums; free catalogue.

Melvin E. Wyant, Rose Specialist Inc., Johnny Cake Ridge (Rt. 84), Mentor, Ohio 44060. Miniature roses; catalogue 25¢.

INDEX